Praise (and otherwise) for

98.6 Degrees:
The Art of Keeping Your Ass Alive!

"Cody Lundin has written an irreverent, no-nonsense survival manual—great reading for outdoor enthusiasts. The advice in *98.6 Degrees* could make the difference between life and death when an unexpected scenario arises during a hunting, fishing, or hiking trip."

—*Suite 101* magazine

"*98.6 Degrees: The Art of Keeping Your Ass Alive!* doesn't just tell you how to survive in the wilderness. It smacks you in the face and insists that you're going to survive!"

—**Alan Dean Foster, *New York Times* best-selling author**

"Cody Lundin is the Pied Piper of outdoor survival skills, a man you'd willingly and cheerfully follow into the woods. In his book, he teaches you how to survive with a precious few tools and most importantly, your wits. His words and wisdom are consciousness-raising and potentially lifesaving. His approach is fun, at times radical, and always eye-opening, so the lessons will sink into even the thickest skull. Heed his advice, for the Piper knows his stuff."

—**Tom Shealey, former executive editor of *Backpacker* magazine**

"My enthusiasm, when recently asked to review a new 'how-to-survive book' wasn't exactly overwhelming! That is until I began to read *98.6 Degrees: The Art of Keeping Your Ass Alive!* As I progressed through the book, my enthusiasm rapidly grew with each turned page. Finally, a book that 'tells it like it is' with no fancy wrappings. As a lifelong survival instructor I have cringed at the 'BS' that is regurgitated in the popular outdoor press and in the many cookie-cutter books that are published on the subject. *98.6* is a breath of fresh air and a hard-hitting, no-nonsense book filled with practical information—reading it might literally save your life!"

—**Peter Kummerfeldt, owner, OutdoorSafe Inc.; member, Wilderness Medical Society; and former Survival, Evasion, Resistance and Escape (SERE) training director for the U.S. Air Force Academy**

"Earthy, philosophical, life-affirming, and pragmatic, *98.6 Degrees: The Art of Keeping Your Ass Alive!* offers far more than practical insights and a tool list for wilderness survival. Staying alive begins with a full understanding of the complex human body/mind survival mechanisms, which Cody Lundin decodes in practical language fortified with rally mantras like 'Remember, your life is worth the fight!' and 'Party On!' Detailing the essential mindset, how to preserve your health, and the safest ways to get home from the worst kind of wilderness crisis, Cody Lundin relies upon our most human attributes—intellect, instinct, and physiology. *98.6* is a life-affirming celebration and a must read—it's your key to backcountry survival when the road or trail ends unexpectedly and a life-threatening predicament ensues."

—Moses Ludel, author of *Jeep Owner's Bible*
and past board member for the national TREAD LIGHTLY! program

"We can't endorse your book, mostly for stylistic reasons . . . the whole gonzo attitude . . . the routine profanity, the plainly sexist illustrations, and the religious stuff . . . would make it problematic for NOLS to have our name supporting this book. Our endorsement just isn't even a question."

—John Gookin, curriculum manager,
National Outdoor Leadership School (NOLS)

"*98.6* is a welcome addition to the world of survival manuals. Cody has gone direct to the core of survival (that many authors of the subject either neglect or relegate to a paragraph—at most a chapter) and has devoted his entire manuscript to staying alive. Unlike other books on survival that devote their contents to skills, tricks, and gadgetry that overwhelm the reader, Cody (1) drives home the basics that kill most people placed in a survival situation, (2) goes on to tell you how to prevent them, and (3) tells you how to achieve the best chance of rescue. Although this book is directed toward the novice, it has loads of information (and presentation quality) that will benefit many of today's survival instructors. Regardless of who the reader is, he/she will come away with an understanding of how to stay alive in the wilderness."

—John McPherson, author of *Naked into the Wilderness,
Primitive Wilderness Living and Survival Skills*

"Since 1961, I've taught people about the outdoors and how to live and survive, especially in winter. From polar regions to the desert and jungles, I've lived off the land, survived, and returned. When it comes to teaching survival, there are talkers and there are doers. Encapsulated within Cody's book is the essence of doing it—coming back alive—no bullshit, no gimmicks, no untried theories. It's attitude that counts and Cody's got it! If death stares me in the face, I want Cody by my side. If he can't be there, give me his book. Get the attitude also, study with Cody!"

—Dr. James C. Halfpenny, president of A Naturalist's World; fellow of the
Explorer's Club; and author of *Winter: An Ecological Handbook*
and *A Field Guide to Mammal Tracking in North America*

"Sorry, but Anglo-Saxon vulgarisms give evidence of lack of imagination and limited vocabulary, and are not to be taken seriously."

—Col. Jeff Cooper (retired), editor-at-large, *Guns & Ammo* magazine

"Survival Knowledge Explained: Get a handle on the problems you could encounter when straying off the beaten path. Stack the deck in your favor by carrying a few essentials (the kit) that can contribute to your comfort, and tell someone when and where to look for you when you are overdue. Drink enough water, get enough sleep, and realize the importance of not letting your body temperature rise or drop from its norm of 98.6, and there is a good chance you will survive long enough (without having to eat) to be rescued even if it takes a month. The rationale behind this—and more—is very well laid out in *98.6 Degrees: The Art of Keeping Your Ass Alive!* It is one of the few refreshing survival manuals that presents a truly modern and updated approach to survival knowledge. How many manuals today delve as much into the importance of sleep and clothing in survival? The psychological aspects of survival as presented by Lundin make more sense than virtually any other survival manual that I have read so far. *98.6* is an outstanding modern survival manual."

—Mors Kochanski, wilderness living skills instructor and author of the Canadian bestseller *Bush Craft: Wilderness Living and Survival Skills*

"Cody does it again! With his rapid-fire, no-holds-barred teaching style, Cody shows you how to live the good life in the wild outdoors. Party On, Dudes! This is not another silly rip-off of how not to do it. Cody has the time-tested skills and knowledge that it takes to get it right. He knows from firsthand experience acquired in the field where it really counts and explains things clearly and accurately, with a showman's timing and scholar's attention to detail. *98.6* is the one book every outdoor traveler needs to memorize!"

—David Wescott, former president, Boulder Outdoor Survival School and author of *Camping in the Old Style*

"Cody does an outstanding job with his vision of survival . . . I've read it over and over and can't say enough positive things for this piece of literature . . . [It's] what we've needed for years."

—Ernie Coffman, ST2, Team Leader, Survival Instructor for OSSA, Rogue Valley Search and Rescue

"In this book Cody has succinctly and 'in your facedly' blown away the often-written extraneous 'BS' and filler info concerning one's absolute, basic physiological, psychological, and material needs in a short-term survival situation. Then he clearly presents the necessary planning and means for being truly prepared. If R. Crumb's late-60s underground comic character Mr. Natural had read this book, then found himself in a real survival situation, I'll bet he'd wisely expound, 'I found the right tool for the job!' Now YOU have too! Plan ahead, keep your wits, and Party On!"

—Jim Riggs, primitive living skills instructor
and author of *Blue Mountain Buckskin*

"I've read or skimmed just about every 'survival' book written since I first started wandering around in the boonies as a pre-teen Boy Scout, and I can't think of anything more boring than yawning and snoring over yet another 'How to Survive in the Woods with Nothing More than a GPS and Cell Phone' by Eddie Expert who copied every chapter from the U.S. Air Force Survival Manual. Anyway, What's this I see? Illustrations by Russ Miller? Actual 'humor' applied to such a 'serious' subject? Irreverence in the face of catastrophe? Poo-pooing the 'experts'? Trying to separate the bull from the bullshit? Son, how dare you flaunt your idiosyncratic ideas and creative approach to such a tried-and-true dull subject. What will all those Rangers, S&R folks, Sheriff's Posses, and other 'experts' think of such a callous approach to keeping one's ass alive? How dare you expect people who venture into the boonies to be responsible for themselves. Don't you know we live in a 'Great Cry-Baby Society' where everyone else is responsible for you and your screw-ups? How dare you expect folks to think for themselves and get themselves out of their own predicaments. Don't you know that thousands of law-school graduates need money and will sue your ass for expecting people to keep their own asses alive? And, to be honest, since I am a bonafide 'expert' on survival myself, I really don't need this book . . . but—maybe I'll just keep this here copy tucked into my survival blanket. I could always use some new ideas, bring it out for a few chuckles under the desert stars. Let's see here . . . hmm . . . hell, this is pretty good writing. It is refreshingly different from the other 'sleeping-pill survival books' I've been forced to read and review. Ya know, maybe I'll order a few more copies for my friends. Hell, maybe I'll even send a few to my enemies."

—Dave Ganci, Rogue Senior, Coyote Face, Ghengis Khan admirer,
Cheap Beer 'Expert,' bona-fide Desert Rat, and author of *The Basic
Essentials of Desert Survival* and *Desert Hiking*

"This book is HOT . . . and, yes, this book is COOL! Mr. Lundin has anchored his survival treatise in the ultimate reality world of those things that push your thermostat too high or too low. Boiling it down to basics, he combines psychology, soul, and sound technique to keep your temperature in the 'live another day' zone. Pay attention mountain, desert, and forest travelers, and you, too, can emerge truly COOL from the most trying of tests . . . survival, with your wits, in a hostile environment."

—Dan Hourihan, President, Mountain Rescue Association (MRA)

98.6 DEGREES

The art of keeping YOUR ASS ALIVE!

CODY LUNDIN

GIBBS SMITH
TO ENRICH AND INSPIRE HUMANKIND
Salt Lake City | Charleston | Santa Fe | Santa Barbara

13 12 11 10   15 14 13 12 11

Text © 2003 by Cody Lundin
Illustrations © 2003 by Russ Miller
Photographs © 2003 by Christopher Marchetti

Reality Check

All survival scenarios by nature are life-threatening. Some of the information presented in this book, if used incorrectly, could help kill you. Anyone
who provides training that guarantees your safety during an outdoor survival situation is either a fool or a liar. Neither the author, the publisher,
nor anyone else assisting in the creation of this book is responsible for your
ultimate fate upon using the material contained within these pages.

Published by
Gibbs Smith, Publisher
P.O. Box 667
Layton, Utah 84041

Orders: (1-800) 748-5439
www.gibbs-smith.com

Edits and cover ass modeling by Suzanne Gibbs Taylor
Designed and produced by Kurt "Nature Boy" Wahlner
Printed and bound in China, land of cheap, small rubber toys

Library of Congress Cataloging-in-Publication Data

Lundin, Cody.
  98.6 degrees: the art of keeping your ass alive / Cody Lundin.—1st ed.
    p. cm.
  ISBN 1-58685-234-5 978-1-58685-234-4
  1. Wilderness survival—Handbooks, manuals, etc. I. Title: Ninety-eight point six
degrees. II. Title.
GV200.5 .L86 2003
613.6'9—dc21
                                        2002152817

Contents

"Good taste is the enemy of creativity."
—PABLO PICASSO

DEDICATION

This book is dedicated to all Beings of Light, seen and unseen, who freely give Their unwavering support and assistance to life. It is my hope that in the not-so-distant future, the concepts herein will no longer be needed as we will live within a conscious under-standing of our true Selves.

ACKNOWLEDGMENTS

This book is a compilation of a part of my life, which has been enriched by too many folks to name. I wish to thank everyone who has crossed my path for sharing your experiences and helping me, even if it was not done consciously. I offer the greatest thanks and gratitude to all the Ascended and Cosmic Ones, to all the Archangels, Archeia, and angels, elementals, and Elohim for being my ultimate survival kit. I owe you my life for protecting me the many times I walked, and sometimes ran, toward death. To Bob and Annabelle and the others who helped me physically by providing several backyards to sleep in, you've helped me to live my dream. To all my survival instructors and students, I hope this book makes you proud, or at least makes you laugh out loud. A whopping "hats off" to Russ "Grog" Miller for his family, friendship, and the outrageous artwork decorating these pages. Without a doubt, good ol' "Miller Magic" played a tremendous role in making this book a destined cult classic. My extreme gratitude goes to Christopher Marchetti for his killer photography. Who would have thunk it, right, man? Much thanks to Yavapai College—especially Jennifer Taylor and the team at the Athletics department for being so helpful and supportive and for the liberal use of the computer. A hearty hug goes to Clint and Nancy Davis and my extended family at Champions Gym for accepting me for who I am, smell and all. Thanks to Georgene and Jim Lockwood for their wisdom, experience, and encouragement, and to the crew at Gibbs Smith, Publisher for their patience and having the balls to do something different. Finally, to my family, my loved ones, and to all those so dear to my heart who believed in me and my process, or at least got out of the way, this book is for you.

FOREWORD

Imagine that you are on a day hike alone and that the unthinkable happens—you fall and break a leg or worse. Because it was just a day hike, you did not tell anyone where you were going and when they should expect you back. The weather is hot and dry—over 100°F during the day, dropping to 50°F at night. Are you equipped to survive? Have you practiced using your emergency gear in difficult situations? Will you survive before help is notified and tries to locate where in the world you are without any clues to help in the process? What you do before the emergency will determine your chance of survival.

Each year thousands of people leave their houses for a day in the outdoors, to hike, snow ski, hunt, or just enjoy being outside. Out of these thousands, many people become injured or lost in the outdoors without being prepared for potential disaster. In each case, volunteer Search and Rescue Team members from across the nation brave the elements to search for, rescue, and, unfortunately, many times recover the remains of a large number of these people who they do not even know.

Even the best outdoorspeople fall victim to Mother Nature, but the majority of these "victims" are not prepared to face the challenges of the outdoors. A few simple preparations before leaving can mean the difference between life and death. *98.6 Degrees: The Art of Keeping Your Ass Alive!* is a must-have book for anyone who enters the "wilderness" for a day hike or extended stay. It provides an honest and simplified lesson on how to survive when "Murphy" strikes and places you in a life-threatening situation.

As the President of the National Association for Search and Rescue (NASAR) I recommend that anyone who ventures into Mother Nature's playground to take the time to learn from Cody Lundin's years of backcountry experience. He has condensed several large "how-to" manuals to a concise work that you can use in your everyday life. His keep-it-simple, useable philosophy works! As an SAR professional, *98.6 Degrees* will be a definite addition to my library and my survival skills.

—MIKE TUTTLE,
PRESIDENT, NATIONAL ASSOCIATION FOR
SEARCH AND RESCUE (NASAR)

CHECK THIS OUT!

 od knows the world doesn't need another book about outdoor survival skills. Many are merely copied from the old Air Force survival manual, are a bore to read, and offer little in the way of original thought or creativity. Even more disturbing are the crappy, pop-culture manuals describing how to wrestle an alligator in four paragraphs or less.

It's a pity that in order to appear "professional" in today's culture, most ideas must be stripped of all life and originality until sterility becomes the only common ground. This mind-set is truly unfortunate and perpetuates a featureless, monoculture landscape with little chance of affecting the world. It doesn't take any guts for someone to applaud when others are already clapping.

The format and style of this book is no accident—it is most likely different from anything you've experienced. While it might not be politically correct, it's designed to help prevent you and your loved ones from coming home in a body bag. I make my living teaching outdoor survival skills. First and foremost, I am an instructor who is convinced that learning doesn't have to be a drag and that a knowledgeable teacher with a fresh, passionate delivery can even make learning fun! Over the years, I've discovered that being a good instructor and a good skills' practitioner are two very different commodities. It's one thing to make fire with sticks, but it is quite another to effectively teach the skill in a way that's memorable. My teaching style is "in your face," filled with poor humor, parlor tricks, and fluctuating voice intonations—anything to obtain and keep the attention of the viewer. I have attempted to write this book in this style. Hopefully, it doesn't lose much in the translation from speech to print.

Since well-oiled memory patterns are vital when assessing and dealing with high-stress situations like those in a true survival scenario, I present material in a very visual nature. I have found that most folks are visual learners. Written languages, respectfully, are fairly new on the scene as all our ancestors at some point drew images or symbols and told stories to communicate. This deep response to symbolism is alive and well in the human psyche and is a very effective means for relaying information *quickly* and *simply*. The old adage "a picture is worth a thousand words" rings true and will continue to do so forever. In essence, teaching images are instinctual and have been the hallmark of successful learning for centuries.

Humor has also been used by teachers to affect students in a deeper way than that of run-of-the-mill, conventional instruction. It's no accident that many of the major world religions and indigenous tribal cultures use the metaphor of humor for its greater impact and memory potential in their learning parables.

A true survival scenario will tax you beyond belief on all levels of your humanity, and one of the first things to go down the toilet will be your fine and complex motor skills—cognitive, physical, and otherwise. Overall, you'll be reduced to basic gross-motor-movement activities and simple "thought pictures." Due to this, if you find yourself in an emergency situation, the visual teachings of Tommy Tardigrade, Willy Nilly, Carmen, Ken Action, Elvis Parsley, and the gang that follow will be with you long after my words are forgotten.

WHY A SURVIVAL KIT?

"I t can't happen to me."

Does this sound familiar? The result of this simple statement is *lack of preparation* and is one of the main reasons people get into a jam in the wilderness. The cause is usually arrogance or ignorance, although the two seem to complement each other nicely.

This book is based upon a lecture I developed many years ago called "Staying Alive: A Basic Approach to Wilderness Survival and the Personal Survival Kit." This lecture simplifies the inner workings of survival situations by focusing on how to prevent and deal with the biggest killers of all outdoor enthusiasts—*hypothermia* and *hyperthermia*—and keep your core body temperature at a lively 98.6°F (37°C).

It's general knowledge that the average person remembers a concept only after being exposed to it six or seven times. Effective survival training stems from natural reactions to critical situations, which is why many core ideas are repeated throughout this book. Curse me if you will for the redundancy, but I'm doing it so these core ideas become natural reactions.

My intention is to provide you with skills and knowledge to help keep you *out* of a "typical" short-term survival situation, and, if all else fails, to provide you with the makings of a good survival kit. This book is *not* meant to be a "field guide." It should be utilized in town to help you prepare *before* heading into the backcountry.

That said, even a casual skimming of these pages should leave little doubt that the wisdom within is not exclusively reserved for a wilderness survival situation.

Ultimately, this book enables you and those you love to become more self-reliant during times of change—any change.

In our current world affairs, knowing what to do and how to do it quickly during emergencies can save your life, whether in the city or in the country. Even better is the ability to read a potentially deadly threat before it occurs, thus avoiding the conflict altogether. These gifts, as well as a resurgence of safety and confidence, are just a few of the benefits of becoming more self-reliant in your world.

Why did I pick a survival kit as the living metaphor for this book?

A survival kit is a distillation of the most simple and effective means of staying alive. It's your lifeline in times of need, the components within possibly being your only chance for living through your present crisis. This book is different from other survival books because it deals exclusively with the outdoor survival kit. While kits are featured in virtually every book, pamphlet, and handout on wilderness survival, they are typically reduced to small token lists of things to carry. This gutless list usually appears in the appendix or some other last-minute spot in the book, rarely offering any information beyond suggesting you carry a pocketknife, matches, rope, and so forth.

I've focused on keeping the kit elements as simple as possible without relying on expensive, hard-to-find specialty gear so you can locate the key items anywhere, from small, mom-and-pop general stores in Oregon to back-forty hardware stores in the Ozark Mountains. Simplicity is the essence of staying alive.

For the average outdoor enthusiast, the components in this kit—along with adequate clothing, water, and a rescue plan—should prove valuable in times of need. Whether you hike, bike, hunt, or camp, this book will help you design a survival kit that's right for your needs—knowing how to use it is up to you.

For most folks, proper preparation and a little bit of luck will keep them out of trouble for years. But, all too often and regardless of prior preparation, a life-threatening situation rears its ugly head. Dozens of people who have lost their lives in the outdoors might still be breathing air if they had a survival kit and the know-how to use it.

My wish for you is that you learn the knowledge contained within these pages without ever having to face the ultimate test.

Primitively Yours,

Cody Lundin, March 2003

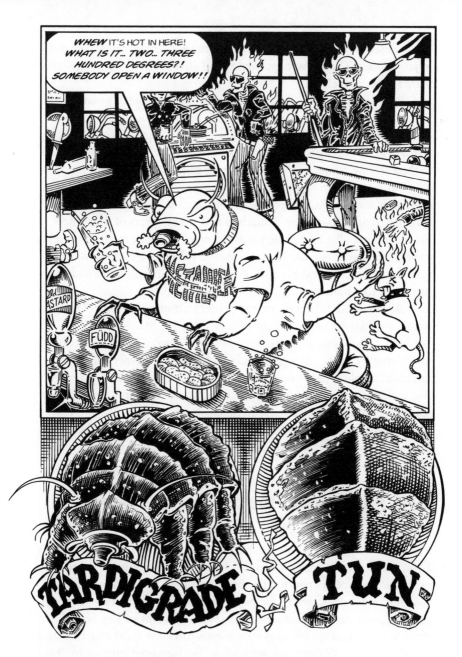

Introducing "Tommy Tardigrade": Faithful sidekick and ultimate survivor!

Tardigrades, a phylum of their own, are microscopic animals around a millimeter in length that live in nearly every habitat on earth—from lake bottoms to the oceans' depths, from moss in the arctic tundra to damp desert sands and high alpine mountains, to the wet leaves stuck in your gutter. They have even been found alive and kicking under more than 16 feet of ice!

Regardless of their lack of size, tardigrades have a mouth, head, brain, legs, eyes, and nerves, and feature precise muscle control, which allows them to move like higher animals. They were nicknamed "little water bears" by August Ephraim Goeze, a German pastor, in 1773, due to their stubby clawed feet and lumbering gait.

Tardigrades are renowned for their ability to survive extreme conditions in a state of suspended animation. In fact, tardigrades have been reanimated after more than a hundred and twenty years of dormancy! In the short term, all a tardigrade needs is water. When life starts to get a bit too dry, the tardigrade draws in its legs and rolls into a ball, transforming itself into a *tun*. Clothed as a tun, its metabolism virtually stops and water loss is cut to a minimum.

Without a doubt, tuns are the planet's ultimate survivor. They can withstand blazing temperatures of 304°F (151°C) to –459°F (–237°C) —which is only one degree above absolute zero! They are also quite unaffected by severe drought, acids and solvents, immersion in liquid nitrogen, alcohol, pressures of nearly 6,000 atmospheres, and radioactive radiation. Add just a drop of water, however, and the little tun rehydrates to form a happy tardigrade.

Since he relies on his tun-like clothing for protection and controls his water loss, Tommy Tardigrade is a stellar reminder of the importance of clothing and water for survival.

Elvis Parsley and the Rest of the Gang

A profound and animated Elvis impersonator, Elvis Parsley was raised in a musical family where, as a small child, he fearlessly fronted his father's Latin polka band "Smooth Move." Later in life, he rose to local fame as the tireless spokesman for the Buttercup Beef Company, a statewide slaughterhouse dedicated to the preservation of lunch meats. After completing his career as a featured regular on the strips of Las Vegas, Mr. Parsley now reserves his impersonation shows for local charities and nursing homes. We were pleased when he answered our ad for help with this project and feel lucky to have someone with his grit, confidence, and experience in the art of active persistence.

Willy Nilly

Although rather nervous, timid, and somewhat confused, Willy Nilly's love and respect for the outdoors far surpassed our expectations. While some may say innocence is blind, Mr. Nilly demonstrates that one is never too seasoned to learn more and continually improve upon one's skills. His lack of ego and bias allows him to excel at listening to others and the subtle wisdoms they share, adapting their knowledge to serve his needs.

Ken Action

Birthed using the marvels of injection-molded plastic technology in 1952, Ken Action caught our attention in the back room of a military surplus store in Rock Springs, Wyoming. His dedication to the facts, thoroughness, and no-nonsense presentation made him a natural for our project when conveying complex terminology and detail-oriented skills. Mr. Action also serves as a valuable liaison and reminder for those too rigid in their thoughts and activities, thereby stifling creativity, humor, and adaptability. Failure to adapt to the current world evolution by remaining a slave to stagnant, outdated teaching and training methodologies breeds mediocrity at best.

Carmen

Carmen has a natural affinity and awareness for the outdoors and is respected for her intuitive knowledge of how nature works. Her leadership style, positive attitude, and warmth help calm the nerves of the others. Although practical, strong, and focused, she balances her intelligence with the needs of the moment, proving that flexibility is a survivor's best friend. She is often approached for sage advice and renders a tremendous service as the glue that holds the other characters together.

SURVIVAL SITUATIONS: HOW DO THEY START?

*H*ow do survival situations happen? How do they start? These are loaded questions. A more accurate one would be, "How *don't* they start?" Murphy's Law, remember? That which can go wrong will. Flat tires, freak weather, wrong turns, broken limbs, and a million more scenarios exist for screwing up in the woods. More often than not, life-threatening affairs are the end result of several seemingly insignificant events. Taken one at a time, they would have little effect, but when compounded they can kill. Therefore, a main part of any survival strategy is to recognize danger signs early so corrective action can be taken.

One of the more common ways to meet your maker is couched innocently enough in the simple day hike. Can you guess why? Have you ever heard someone say, "Ain't nothin' gonna happen, honey. We'll only be gone for a few hours. It's just a day hike!"

Day hikes are notorious for compromising lives because they lull people into a sense of complacency in regard to properly preparing for a trip. Phrases like "We don't need that extra sweater," or "Leave the water in the truck!" can end up putting people six feet under.

Many people have died less than a mile from their vehicles without even being in the wilderness.

A few years ago, in the Arizona desert, an elderly couple made a wrong turn in their car and found themselves traveling a dirt road on the outskirts of Phoenix. After getting stuck in a sand wash, the woman abandoned ship to walk toward a major interstate that was clearly in view. A few days later, searchers found her body less than a mile from the highway, dead from dehydration and hyperthermia. Her frail husband, who stayed with the car, died as well. A rearview mirror dislodged from the vehicle and aimed at highway traffic might have brought help their way. What a terrible waste. Proper preparation can save your life—ask anyone who's died of exposure; they'll tell you.

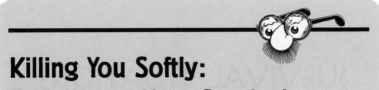

Killing You Softly:
Enemies to Your Survival

While it's impossible to complete this list due to the infinite variables present within human nature and Mother Nature, many outdoor travelers commonly face the enemies below. While there are no guarantees in a survival situation, proper planning, coupled with quality survival training and subsequent practice, will prevent many of these from occurring in the first place.

- Anxiety and fear (these two, when mixed with the power of the imagination, are voracious killers)
- Pain and injury
- Illness
- Cold and heat
- Thirst and hunger
- Wetness
- Fatigue and sleep deprivation
- Boredom
- Loneliness and isolation
- Complacency and the desire for comfort
- Stubbornness (refusal to recognize and stop actions jeopardizing survival)
- Promises (unrealistic guarantees made to self or others leading to stupid behavior)
- "Get-home-itis" (setting and trying to maintain unrealistic time lines)

The last three enemies often subtly work their infectious death magic together, slowly, but surely, eroding away your good judgment.

SURVIVAL VS. PRIMITIVE LIVING, OR "LIVING OFF THE LAND"

If you fail to get you and your loved ones out of a modern survival sce-nario, you will all die. It's not like the bar is closing at 1:00 A.M. and you're down to your last six-pack, or getting a flat tire three blocks from home. It's a serious life-threatening situation with little regard for the environment or anything else. You may resort to felling live trees, burning obnoxious petroleum products, or un-daintily harvesting materi-als necessary to keep you and those you love alive. You will be subjected to tremendous mental, emotional, and physical stress. You will need to strictly abide by the laws of how the body loses and gains heat through conduction, convection, radiation, evaporation, and respiration. Often, unless blessed by a favorable event during your survival ordeal, you won't be given a second chance if you blow it.

There are very few rules, but your main goals are to regulate core body temperature and get rescued from your predicament as soon as possible.

The Modern Survival Scenario

Survival situations come in as many shapes and sizes as there are zits on a teenager, and can last for various periods of time. You can be dead in a couple of minutes, hours, days, weeks, or months. However, *the average survival scenario lasts for 72 hours, or three days*. Statistically speaking, this is the amount of time that passes before searchers find you dead or alive—as long as you have someone searching for you. The whole focus of this book is betting on the fact that you'll be rescued within a three-day time period—largely because you bothered to tell someone where you were going. This obviously does not mean that you should give up if your predicament lasts longer, but instead means you will have to try even harder. Never give up trying to survive. If you become compromised in the woods today, the chances are high that you'll fall into the modern survival category.

Primitive Living

A primitive living situation is a long-term commitment. There is no getting rescued because you're already home. If you find yourself in this situation, chances are your uncle is wearing a buckskin loincloth chewing on a piece of dried pack-rat meat.

Differences

There is much confusion regarding the difference between a modern survival scenario and primitive living skills. They are two completely different scenarios whose main objectives overlap: the main objective in each is to stay alive, one short-term (statistically) and one long-term. For the average outdoor recreationist, primitive skills should take a backseat to learning modern survival skills if learning to survive is the main intention. In other words, discover the magic of making fire by friction after you perfect using matches.

In any event, all modern survival skills originated from primitive skills, and the beauty of knowing both is empowering. If I lose my knife, I can make one from stone. If my magnesium and matches go down the river, I have the potential to create fire with sticks.

To effectively teach modern survival skills, one should be well-versed in primitive skills as well. Nothing imparts the mind-set of being able to do more with less and the possibilities of improvisation like living primitively. Like everything else, however, times change and with that change comes an array of modern goodies that can prove valuable to your survival.

I attended a gathering several years ago and watched a friend and renowned primitive skills instructor use nearly an entire book of matches to light a fire. This same person can make a fire with sticks in less than twenty seconds. Learning survival skills is much the same as learning martial arts. Would you rather face an assailant with a half a dozen throwing stars or an Uzi? Modern-day samurai warriors would certainly carry a full arsenal of automatic weaponry and other technological gizmos. There is an old saying, "Don't carry a knife to a gun fight," especially if you have a choice in the matter! With the samurai, only the look of the tool has evolved over time, but the *intention* behind the tool—the warrior mind-set, physical training, and common sense—has essentially remained the same.

One of the main illusions confusing a primitive situation and a modern one is the importance of food. Remember, the average modern survival scenario lasts three days or less. I know people who have fasted for forty days and none of them were named Jesus. In fact, a normal well-nourished adult has sufficient fat stores to live for sixty to seventy days, albeit in a controlled clinical setting. Soldiers in the field, when subjected to serious food restrictions have routinely maintained a relatively normal workload for up to nine days. During World War II, the well-known Minnesota starvation studies found that a loss of less than 10-percent body weight did not impair physical performance. It was only when the subject continued the starvation pattern for longer periods of time and lost more body weight that physical performance began to nose-dive.

Teaching a basic survival class how to catch food with a variety of traps and snares is not only unrealistic and impractical (imagine your urban sixty-year-old aunt setting up scores of dead-fall traps), it ignores the more important issue of regulating body temperature. Besides, unless you trap for a living, your chances of harvesting more calories than you'll use dinking around is debatable. In extreme cold weather, food would be nice since digestion generates metabolic heat, but it doesn't replace the hat and parka. Most of us have ample calories stored around our waist to get us through the most compromising modern situations.

98.6 Degrees: The Art of Keeping Your Ass Alive!

SURVIVAL PSYCHOLOGY AND THE IMPORTANCE OF PROPER PRIOR TRAINING

"Rule your mind or it will rule you."

—HORACE

Survival is 90 percent psychology. When the chips are down, it doesn't matter what you have buried in the backyard or how many books on survival you've read. If you're a mental and emotional basket case during your survival episode, you're toast.

The benefits of a positive attitude are many, and they range from improving your health and aiding disease resistance to putting more cash in your bank account. Science has proven that attitude, self-esteem, and humor influence changes in heart rate, hormones, and body chemistry. All living cells respond instantaneously to every thought and feeling we have. Like donning a pair of colored glasses, how we think and feel about the world affects our perception about everyone and everything. If the world looks like hell to someone, so be it. For that person it turns out to be just that. Another person will experience the world as blissful; and so it is, at least for him or her. Put another way, your psychology creates your physiology.

Training in the physical skills necessary to survive is rather easy when compared to the psychological aspect of survival. People who die in survival situations experience psychological death long before their physical bodies check out. Fear, anxiety, embarrassment, anger, frustration, guilt, depression, confusion, boredom, and loneliness are common reactions to emergency stress. All will attempt to strip you of hope, coercing you into giving up the fight for life. As we will soon explore, in life-threatening situations, the line between a survivor's physiological and psychological responses becomes rather transparent.

A friend of mine is a police officer on the local SWAT team. At times he'll get a call in the middle of the night about a hostage situation to which he immediately responds. Once there, he reports to the commanding officer, who issues him a specialized weapon. On one particular evening, the magazine cartridge for the rifle is wrapped with blue tape instead of red. Instantly his adrenaline plummets. It's a drill. There is no hostage predicament. Every movement for the rest of this night, while valuable, couldn't possibly compare to the adrenaline rush before seeing blue tape wrapped around the magazine.

Prior training for the unexpected emergency is a wise move. It has been proven that repeatedly practicing something makes a deeper and deeper groove within the limbic system, a system which commands certain behaviors necessary for the survival of all mammals. Physiologically, practice makes perfect, or pretty darn close.

Put Up or Shut Up

All people thrust into a survival situation go through the process of identifying the particular threat or threats and then formulating a plan to deal with them. The amount of time you have to go through the steps below is dependent upon what's happening. Your reaction to the scenario might happen in a few seconds (grizzly bear charge) or days, and will continuously fluctuate as more and more information about your predicament is revealed.

Reaction to the scenario:

1. Recognition phase.
2. Speed (body functions react: blood pressure increases, heart rate quickens, etc.).
3. Adaptation or nonadaptation (fainting).
4. Steps taken for survival.

The increased proficiency developed through practice cuts down on the *reaction time* needed to perform a skill, thus using a lot less energy. This last point is critical since you will not always have just gulped down a heaping bowl of cereal and awakened refreshed from ten hours of beauty rest when the emergency begins. You will usually be ragged around the edges and unraveling fast with few supplies to help ward off death.

Scientific studies regarding *learning* and *memory* point directly to the neurons of the brain. An adult human brain contains approximately 12 to 15 billion nerve cells, of which we use a paltry 4 percent of its potential. Like a biological dating game, these neurons, or tiny information processing cells, hang out and attempt to make connections with other neurons. Many are quite good at this, as some individual neuron connections number in the thousands. The more the brain is "used," the more connections are made and the higher your SAT scores are. Dendrites, tiny tree-like structures, use their many branches to funnel electrical signals into the neurons themselves. When the proper signal trips the neurons' trigger so to speak—and not all of them do—the neuron sends its own message down a stalk-shaped axon. The axon funnels the information through junctions called synapses, which then lead to the dendrites of other cells.

Memory, the act of recall and recognition, is based upon two variables. One involves how many senses (sight, sound, smell, touch, and taste) are involved to stimulate the remembering. The more senses that are brought into play, the greater the memory. The other variable assists in forming the pattern for the memory itself. Memory involves repeated firings between dendrites. When a new skill is acquired, the fresh information has a hell of a time jumping the synaptic gap between dendrites. There's no pattern to follow, no well-worn path, as the skill has embarked upon "the road never traveled." The first time a new skill is learned and a connection between dendrites made, the brain releases a slippery, fatty protein called myelin. Initially, like a newly intimate couple in desperate need of lubricant, the new information has a rough time crossing over. Each time the connection is activated, however, more slippery myelin coats the dendrites, until eventually, with enough practice and repetition, the connection is fully lubed and can operate quickly with minimal effort. **The more survival skills an individual has that have been practiced physically and otherwise, the better odds they have for those skills coming to the forefront during a stressful emergency.** For the survivor, multiple, thoroughly lubricated myelin connections preprogram decisive, speedy solutions to deadly scenarios by directly dropping critical motor movement patterns into the central nervous system.

While the quest for perfection can kill you quickly in the outdoors, accomplishing a skill well is a real confidence builder. This calming confidence penetrates deep within the individual, past the conscious mind, allowing the person to get into action quickly during crisis situations, minimizing the potential for "freeze ups." Freeze ups, becoming immobilized by fear and panic, typically result from experiencing a threat that is perceived as beyond the ability of the perceiver to effectively deal with.

> *"It is not so much what you believe in that matters, as the way in which you believe it and proceed to translate that belief into action."*
> —LIN YUTANG

Situations are stressful to people because they see them as so. To some, going without toilet paper in the wilderness pushes major buttons. Having never wiped their butt with a rock, stick, or other natural nicety, new synapses must be created on the spot.

All perceptions can be altered with proper training and subsequent practice. Practice reduces response time, which in itself might save your life. Mother Nature is full of variation—variation that may give way to fear or panic if left unchecked. The more mock situations you put yourself through, the better adapted you'll be to real-time stress.

Scads of incidents point to the fact that those who mentally and physically rehearse emergency procedures benefit from automatic action when a crisis occurs. *Imagery* has been used for as long as there have been people. When building a house, you produce an image in your mind about how you'd like the house to look. This information is given to an architect who then makes the image tangible on paper. The image is then filled with the power of emotion and sweat equity and—Wham!—the building manifests itself from thin air. Mental imaging, used by top athletes for decades, strengthens the motor programs of whatever you visualize in your head through low-level stimulation of the muscle fibers involved. The action of striking a match for instance, can be improved upon by properly striking the match as a moving image in your mind. Playing out what-if survival scenarios, and the correct reactions to them, have an equal value. Visualizing a number of correct reactions provides options while further boosting confidence. In other words, mental practice, to a point, further greases the synapses between dendrites.

The Ten (Eleven) Essentials

Although generic in its format, the following list, usually referred to as "The Ten Essentials," highlights the skills and know-how any trained outdoors person should possess. While lacking in its advice regarding hot temperatures, and the importance of adequate sleep, which I've added as number eleven, the list's overall effectiveness is proven and timeless in its application.

1. A positive attitude.
2. Fuel to burn: food.
3. Adequate hydration: water.
4. Ability to stay warm and dry: clothing.
5. Ability to get dry: shelter.
6. Ability to get warm: fire.
7. Know where you are going: navigation.
8. Know the environment: weather.
9. Ability to attract help: signaling for rescue.
10. Ability to provide help: first-aid kit.
11. Ability to obtain physiological and psychological repair: adequate sleep.

The inarguable bottom line is this: regardless of how simple a skill appears on the surface, *all conscious body actions are composed of extremely complex neurophysiological functions.* It is imperative that you keep your survival plans as simple as possible. Fancy, complicated, hard-to-learn skills represented in many survival books and videos, and the junk they try to sell, flat out have no relevance in a real-time, modern-field emergency.

All professional survival instructors have consciously chosen the profound responsibility of training their clients to effectively and efficiently deal with deadly worst-case scenarios. It is not just another job or fun hobby. With this responsibility comes the obligation to understand how the human body reacts to and deals with stress, whether through hot and cold weather, fear, panic, or a billion and more scenarios Mother Nature and human nature can dish out. Teaching tactics

(catch the rest on page 32)

Sweet Dreams

The importance of getting a good night's sleep cannot be overemphasized. Like oxygen, water, and food, sleep is an essential physiological need. The relationship between sleepiness and accidents has long been apparent, from taking a wrong turn in the woods to the horrors of Three Mile Island, Chernobyl, and the Exxon *Valdez*. Athletes the world over have long believed in the power of shut-eye for optimal performance. Studies on sleep deprivation, both military and civilian, are prolific yet there's still a lot to know regarding how we spend a third of our life.

In a nutshell, sleep patterns consist of an inactive slow-wave state called *non-REM* and an active dreaming state called *REM,* although there are tons of age-related differences in sleep patterns. Both are regulated by circadian and homeostatic influences, controlled by areas of the brain located in the hypothalamus, basal forebrain, and pontine brainstem. *Circadian rhythms,* biological rhythms that occur at an interval of approximately 24 hours, also influence important survival systems such as mental and visual alertness and core body temperature. Even single cells are capable of demonstrating circadian rhythms, which are rhythms that persist regardless of how much sleep, food, or activity you've indulged in. These rhythms systematically and naturally drop core body temperature, whether you have hypothermia or not, and can, for obvious reasons, add fuel to an already ugly predicament as well as can be linked to your metabolism and oxygen use.

While there's much disagreement in the literature, sleep deprivation compromises the body in many ways. It doesn't take a scientific study to realize that a failure to catch some Zs makes folks feel cranky, tired, forgetful, clumsy, and generally no fun to be around. Unfamiliar outdoor stressors, such as strange noises, temperature extremes, calorie deprivation, odd sleep times, and more, work in unison to gradually pound you into submission with a feeling of extreme fatigue and weariness. Although most of what we know about the lack of sleep revolves around the immune system and brain function, sleep deprivation was recently found to interfere with the metabolism of glucose (a critical source of energy for all cellular activity) by slowing it down 30 to 40 percent! This could impair endurance, physical recovery time, and the regulation of body temperature. The storage of glucose in the muscles and liver (glycogen) is particularly important for any endurance activity. In a sleep -deprived state, glycogen storage may be slowed, preventing the survivor from "topping off the gas tank." Elevated levels of the stress hormone cortisol, a catabolic (breakdown) hormone, were also discovered and have been linked to the development of memory impairments, impaired tissue repair and growth, and a depressed immune system, causing greater susceptibility to nasty cold bugs and diseases. While tasks that require a short burst of concentration are less affected from weariness, tasks that require constant monitoring— like looking for your rescuers—suffer big time. In addition, outside of practiced skills, complex decision-making plummets as does short-term memory and verbal communication. On the plus side, oddly enough, sleep deprivation has been used as an alternative treatment for depression, producing drastic improvements in the moods of about 60 percent of the people who tried it.

The good news is that the negative effects of sleep deprivation can be cured by a normal sleep pattern. Much evidence also points to the fact that "strong motivation," paired with good physical conditioning, is one of the principal factors for temporarily holding at bay the effects of fatigue. The bottom line is that the jury is still out on many aspects of sleep-deprivation physiology, and more studies need to be accomplished before any "new" information sticks.

Equally important, if not more important for the survivor, is the ability to stay awake if necessary when tired. Try stimulation activities such as movement, conversation, drinking, chewing, or anything else you can think of to help temporarily shake the sleepies. If you're up for a challenge, the world record for not sleeping in a person without a medical condition is 18 days and 17 hours.

The All-Powerful Nap

Although many scenarios exist that are virtually impossible to sleep through, strive to get as much sleep as you can, when you can. Humans require about 7 to 8 hours of sleep each night depending on age and other individual factors, yet research has shown the importance of achieving a minimum of $4\,1/2$ to $5\,1/2$ hours of "core sleep" every 24 hours. Under the bizarre sleep circumstances of most survival situations, naps may be one of the most effective means of increasing mental, emotional, and physical performance. While naps can be taken at any time, those initiated at night, early morning, and mid-afternoon will allow you to conk out the fastest. The longer the nap, the greater the restorative response, yet naps as short as 20 minutes have been found to be amazingly effective. Snoozing ahead of time, before an expected no-sleep adventure, is also helpful. The well-known nap side effect called *sleep inertia*, or sleep drunkenness, in which you feel bitchy, confused, disoriented, and overall worse than when you started, is easily dealt with by walking around for 5 or 10 minutes after awakening. The moral of the story is obvious, try to avoid doing critical tasks immediately upon waking from a nap.

must be sought that consciously and subconsciously prepare a student for the real-world pressures of staying alive by allowing the student to actualize basic skills quickly with a limited response time. Repetitious, realistic training—based upon simple, gross motor skills that are easy to learn, practice, and perform—does wonders for a student's motivation and confidence. Once an instructor understands the physiology of how freaked-out people react and what they can be expected to accomplish physically, mentally, and emotionally, the instructor can develop and teach skills and activities that are relevant and effective in a modern, short-term survival emergency.

Even the most experienced outdoors person can and does get caught off guard, so don't expect to be a superman or woman. Nature has a way of opening your Pandora's box, regardless of your level of training. Like my friend's SWAT scenario earlier, 100 percent training realism in understanding the effects of intense mental and emotional stress is impossible to obtain. Regardless of the quality of training and the competence of the instructors, the student always knows it's a drill. This knowledge is a personal blind spot into our own psychology. The reality of your survivor mind-set is this: while training is a must and of extreme value, you'll never truly know what you're made of until the day the brown stuff hits the fan.

WHY FEAR SUCKS

"If you are scared, you will die."
—RICHARD VAN PHAM,
AFTER BEING RESCUED BY A U.S. WARSHIP AFTER
SPENDING THREE MONTHS ADRIFT AT SEA. ASIDE
FROM HAVING A POSITIVE ATTITUDE, RICHARD
SURVIVED BY CATCHING RAINWATER AND ROAST-
ING SEA BIRDS THAT LANDED ON HIS SAILBOAT.

While the body's initial response to fear has saved countless lives since time began, the long-term stress of fear sucks, as its damage to the human body has been clinically proven for decades. When the brain perceives a threat to survival, the *sympathetic nervous system* (SNS) goes hog-wild by immediately releasing tons of stress hormones—called adrenaline or epinephrine—into the circulatory system. This reflex action to stress happens automatically and is virtually uncontrollable. The chemical cocktail is the basis for the body's fight-or-flight mechanism and is characterized by several factors, including an increased heart rate (from 70 beats per minute to more than 200 in less than one second), increased cardiac output, higher blood pressure, and increased blood sugar. Blood is diverted from organs to the larger muscle groups, resulting in increased strength capabilities and enhanced gross motor skills while the breathing rate accelerates, thereby transporting greater amounts of oxygen to the newly recruited muscle fibers. At the same time, sweating increases to cool the muscles. Minor blood vessels in the arms and legs constrict to reduce bleeding from potential injuries, digestion ceases, and muscle tremors take over. The pupils dilate, reducing depth perception, while axillary muscle performance takes a nosedive, creating blurred vision. And, as if this isn't enough, the field of sight narrows, producing tunnel vision. To a greater or lesser extent, time appears to pass more slowly, called the tache-psyche effect, allowing for increased reaction time to the perceived emergency.

Researchers have spent years figuring out why stress deteriorates performance in combat soldiers, ultimately linking an elevated heart rate to the crappy execution of fine and complex motor skills. They found that a heart rate of 115 beats per minute or faster severely compromised fine motor skills. When the heart rate exceeded 145 beats per minute, complex motor skills began to suffer. In contrast, in times of high stress, gross motor skills were relatively unaffected! Again, all the more reason to keep your outdoor skills and the gear you carry simple in design.

Once the physiological chaos begins, the SNS rules the body with an iron fist, controlling all voluntary and involuntary systems until the survival threat has been eliminated, personal performance takes a dump, or the *parasympathetic nervous system* (PNS) regains control. The more freaked out you are, the more your SNS takes over your world. Before busting down the door in the middle of the night, police officers on a raid routinely experience low levels of SNS activity, resulting in increased heart rate and respiration, muscle tremors, and a heightened sense of anxiety. Being charged by a grizzly bear, however, will cause very high levels of SNS action due to the qualities of "in your face" potential death coupled with decreased response time. Such cir-

Five Factors Dictating the Severity of an SNS Total Body Takeover

1. The severity of the perceived threat.
2. The time available to respond.
3. Personal confidence in skills and training.
4. The level of experience in dealing with the threat.
5. The amount of physical fatigue combined with the present anxiety.

98.6 Degrees: The Art of Keeping Your Ass Alive!

How Fear
Affects Your Body

A: Constricted Minor Blood Vessels.

B: Dilated Pupils.

C: Increased Breathing Rate.

D: Increased Sweating.

E: Increased Heart Rate Dumps Adrenaline
   into Circulatory System.

F: Digestion Ceases.

G: Loss of Bowel Control.

H: Blood Diverted to Larger
   Muscle Groups.

cumstances cause extreme failure of the body's visual, cognitive, and motor-control systems.

Additional problems surface upon realizing the body's physiological response to extreme stress and the PNS payback time occurring as a result of the demands placed upon it. The SNS mobilizes body resources to deal with the perceived survival scenario. It is the body's "physiological warrior," instantly heading to the front lines for battle regardless of your opinion. The PNS deals with your body's digestive system and its recuperative processes. It is the physiological equivalent of the body's nurturing caretaker, accomplishing everyday tasks for the moment and the future.

When your body is subjected to stress, the natural balance between the two nervous systems goes down the tubes and the physiological warrior starts to raise hell (fight-or-flight mechanism). As the body's energy is redirected to ensure its survival, its caretaker is thrown into battle as well, and nonessential PNS activities suddenly take a dump (sometimes literally). As a result of the PNS shutdown, thousands of World War II veterans admitted to urinating or defecating in their pants during combat operations.

It's a lot of work for the body to maintain such an intense state of alert. At the end of the crisis, the PNS demands attention and the physiological payback commences in the form of feeling amazingly whipped on all levels. But wait, that's not all. A survival situation is a *continuous* roller-coaster of ups and downs, thus the hapless survivor is a slave to repeated chemical cocktails of intense adrenaline spikes and their PNS paybacks. Bit by bit, the body's once-natural and useful response to danger starts to chemically wear down the survivor, pitching the person into a state of immense physical, emotional, and mental exhaustion. In summary, human beings have three primary survival systems: visual, cognitive processing, and motor-skill performance. Under stress, all three go to hell in a handbasket.

The physiological responses to stress can be broken down into four crucial factors for the survivor:

1. *Fear inhibits your metabolic process.* Your body produces heat by digesting the calories in the foods you eat. If this is impaired, your body has a harder time regulating core temperature in cold weather. Thus, the onset of hypothermia can manifest much more rapidly. By metabolizing food, your body creates energy that can be used to create shelter, signal for rescue, or make a fire.

2. *Fear impairs your circulation.* Basic first-aid training stresses

98.6 Degrees: The Art of Keeping Your Ass Alive!

the importance of the ABCs (airway, breathing, and circulation). Your circulatory system is how your body feeds itself, delivers oxygen to cells, eliminates waste products, and keeps itself warm and cool. In cold weather, blood flow is the primary means by which your body maintains its peripheral temperature, which is automatically restricted by the SNS's response to stress! Compromising circulation puts your odds for living into a serious tailspin in both hot and cold climates. In addition, the chances are good that your circulatory system will already be impaired due to dehydration.

3. *Fear impairs your good judgment.* Good judgment is your number-one tool for preventing or dealing with a survival predicament in the first place. **Poor judgment calls, without a doubt, are the hallmark of every single outdoor fatality.** Occurrences such as auditory exclusion, tunnel vision, irrational behavior, freezing in place, and the inability to think clearly have all been observed as by-products of survival stress. Do all you can to chill out and calm yourself, redirecting your energies away from the fear factors.

4. *Fear impairs your fine and complex motor skills.* Although these phenomena have been observed and documented for hundreds of years, and formally studied since the late 1800s, there is very little understanding by researchers as to why stress deteriorates performance.

There are three generic classifications of motor movements or skills involving coordinated action from your body. They are *gross, fine,* and *complex motor skills.* Gross motor movements signify action involving the larger muscle groups of the body, such as the arms and legs. Running, jumping, pushing, pulling, and punching are some examples. Fine motor skills involve some type of "hand-eye" coordination, such as threading a needle or making a ten-foot, Tibetan Buddhist sand mandala. Complex motor skills comprise a whole string or series of motor movements, such as shooting a bow and arrow on horseback at full gallop, or purchasing several copies of this book. The problem lies in the fact that fine and complex motor skills deteriorate rapidly under stress. Highly detailed activities, such as striking a match, become nearly impossible to perform under psychological pressure and the physiological flow of adrenaline, rendering all but the simplest of tasks out of the question. Once the proverbial bullets start to fly, the survivor stops thinking with his or her forebrain, the part that makes us human, and instead depends on the "mid" or mammalian brain, the primitive part of the brain that's unrecognizable from that of an animal.

In contrast, gross motor skills are performed very well under extreme stress and are easier and quicker to learn, often taking just a few minutes of practice to begin forming a motor pattern. For this reason and others, pack survival gear that is simple in design—gear that can be operated using gross motor movements. For example, a magnesium bar with striking insert—a fire-making tool we will explore later—can be crudely scraped into tinder to start a fire. Doing so is much easier to perform under stress than striking a match. Unfortunately, much survival training ignores this fundamental truth by continuing to promote complex, detail-oriented skills and behaviors that have little application in a real-life emergency. These training mistakes are many times responsible for a student's failure to use what he or she has learned when faced with a hairy situation.

Note that two of the four impairments involve basic body temperature regulation. As I've said before, the biggest people killer in the outdoors is exposure, or the failure to regulate core body temperature. It's long been a cliché that fear kills, and now you know why.

Knowledge and practice is power. The more training you have dealing with situations that could jeopardize your life, the more efficiently you'll act if placed in that situation.

Physical and Psychological Fear Factors

While the reactions to fear and anxiety are largely the same, anxiety is usually not as intense as fear and persists for a longer length of time, leading up to a specific threat or fear.

Physical symptoms of fear:

Increased heart rate
Shortness of breath
Tightness in chest and throat
Dry mouth, higher pitched voice, stammering
Increased muscular tension, trembling, and weakness
Sweaty palms, hands, soles of the feet and armpits
Dilated pupils
"Butterflies in the stomach" (hollowness), faintness,
     and nausea
Oversensitivity to noise

Psychological symptoms of fear:

Shock, numbness, denial, helplessness
Confusion, forgetfulness, and the inability to concentrate
Irritability, hostility or passivity, stupor
Talkativeness leading to speechlessness
Restlessness
Panic, flight
Feelings of unreality, social withdrawal, and
     depersonalization
Sadness, crying, sighing
Auditory and visual hallucinations
Disrupted sleep and appetite

Helpful Hints for Dealing with and Controlling Fear

Reading other people's true survival stories is all the proof you'll need that when the going gets tough the tough get going. Throughout history, people have dealt with and surmounted virtually every possible fear imagined. For optimal results in the field or the city, work at cultivating the following tips until the behavior becomes a natural, automatic reaction.

Controlling Fear in Yourself:

1. *Be prepared.* Accept the fact that a survival situation could, in fact, happen to you, and plan accordingly. Aside from physical practice, being prepared involves advanced planning, mental and physical conditioning, discipline, and an intimate understanding of the emergency gear you propose to carry.
2. *Train!* Accepting that a deadly scenario could happen is not enough. Learn all that you can about survival and what your body can endure, and recognize and understand what your reactions to fear will be. Practicing skills builds confidence and strengthens a "can-do" attitude regarding your ability to survive.
3. *Don't run from fear.* When you're afraid, take a step back from the fear and just notice it. Ignore the urge to analyze, judge, criticize, evaluate, or try to figure it out. Stepping back provides emotional space and reduces much of the charge around the fear energy.
4. *Stay aware of your surroundings.* Learn to recognize the early warning signs of dangerous situations. Gain knowledge to reduce the perceived threat of the unknown.
5. *Stay constructively busy.* Conserving energy as a survivor is key, yet do all that you can to make your situation more comfortable, reducing difficulties that encourage fear. Staying busy keeps the mind off fearful circumstances and gives you a sense that you're in control of your destiny.
6. *Keep your imagination in check.* Stick to the known facts by separating the real from the imagined.
7. *Adapt to your surroundings.* Prepare yourself to think and act like

an animal without judgment over your actions. In a sense, if you can't beat fear, join it. Formulate plans B, C, and D before they're needed.

8. *Discipline yourself to think positively.* Even when talking to yourself, strive to use positive, "I AM" statements such as, "I AM going to make it out of here" and "I AM going to be rescued."

9. *Adopt a positive survival attitude.* Keep things in perspective and focus your attention firmly upon the goal of getting rescued.

10. *Use proper breathing exercises to lower the heart rate and reduce stress.* (See exercise on page 55)

11. *Ask for help.* Whether you're currently walking upon a spiritual path or not, it's never too late to start.

12. *Use humor.* Kind humor transforms crummy attitudes.

13. *In summary, Party On!*

Controlling Fear in Others:

1. *Be a positive example.* Maintain a calm presence and keep control, even if you feel out of control; inspire courage, hope, and the willingness to keep trying.

2. *Maintain discipline.* Work toward finding and maintaining order and harmony within the group in a gentle, yet firm manner. Search out people's strengths and assign them focused tasks to assist the group. Giving people things to do lessens feelings of helplessness, and takes their mind away from the current situation, while giving them a sense of control regarding their destiny.

3. *Exercise positive leadership.* Be firm, determined, confident, compassionate, decisive, honest, and humorous.

4. *Stay alert for early signs of fear in others, and, when recognized, deal with them immediately.* Knowing how the people in your group react to and deal with stress is priceless. Be intuitive to the needs of others and offer whatever support you can. Remember that one rotten apple can spoil the bunch.

5. *Cultivate teamwork and mutual support early on.* Perhaps no other experience on Earth will require such a tightly knit and supportive group for success than the survival situation. The group that initiates and maintains a positive mental and emotional outlook, putting all of its efforts and concerns into the welfare of the entire tribe, is an extremely powerful force for staying alive.

6. *In summary, Party On!*

DEALING WITH THE SURVIVAL SCENARIO: ATTITUDE, ADAPTATION, AND AWARENESS

"Those who gave up died."
—DANIEL FERNANDEZ,
ONE OF 16 SURVIVORS FROM THE DOOMED,
1972 URUGUAYAN FLIGHT THAT CRASHED IN THE
ANDES MOUNTAINS. DANIEL AND OTHERS WERE
FORCED TO EAT THE FLESH OF THEIR DEAD
FRIENDS FOR 72 DAYS IN ORDER TO LIVE.

Give up and die. Emergency scenarios from around the globe are rich with examples supporting this painfully simple statement. The following sacred words, borrowed from Desert Rat Dave Ganci, are vital to the survivor: attitude, adaptation, and awareness. Cultivating their attributes will allow you to face obstacles within a positive light. Remember, however, that there are no guarantees that you'll live. Anyone who tells you differently, who guarantees your safety, especially if they stand to make some cash, should be treated either as untruthful or as someone who has forgotten (or has never known) how all-powerful Mother Nature can be.

Attitude

The king of them all is attitude. Maintaining a positive attitude or "will to live" is critical to your survival. If your attitude falls, you'll fall with it. Cultivating a good attitude doesn't mean you have to don flowers and sport a poop-eating grin seven days a week. However, inherent to a positive attitude is the willingness to *try*; and if there is failure, the willingness to try again and again. Researching real-life stories of survivors and the horrific ordeals they've gone through and defeated will put your backcountry crisis into its proper perspective. This knowledge supports a "Yes I Can" attitude essential to your well-being and the others in your group. As a bonus, maintaining a positive outlook is contagious and will cause life in general to become more pleasant. When challenges do arise, they can be dealt with more easily.

Prior training in survival skills boosts confidence and improves your actions under stress. This prior training is proof in itself that you value life in general, especially yours and the ones you love. It's proof that you've taken the time to gain what skills you could to help deal with a life-threatening crisis. It increases self-confidence and causes you to believe that you, in fact, can survive because you've consciously taken the time to acquire the tools to do so. Remember, your life is worth the fight. Of all the millions of people on this planet, only you can accomplish the special tasks you've been given by life. Only you have the power to give your gift back to life for the benefit of us all. Never give up. Although it's important that you carry a positive attitude, it doesn't replace the need for you to carry a well-designed survival kit.

Cultivating Rational Insanity and the Art of "Party On"...Understanding the Psychological Dynamics Behind This Mystical, Magical Mantra

I like to listen to loud heavy-metal music. At some point, headphones blaring, I was given a revelation about cultivating a survivor mind-set. The term that came to me was "rational insanity."

During a survival episode, you'll be taxed to the limit on all levels. In order to prevail and mitigate the panic factor, you'll have to be as cool as a cucumber. You'll need to approach your situation in a somewhat detached and rational manner, while gearing up your mind and body to accomplish the insane if necessary, thereby smashing all self-imposed limitations. Funneling the intense energy of insanity and *uniting it* with the sound coolness of rational decision making creates a potent force in emergency scenarios. Condensing this potency can

best be summed up in one simple statement: the clarion call "Party On!" Remember it in your time of need or whenever you need a boost of courage or focus. Relish and relax in its splendor. It is the most optimistic statement in the world, one in which there is no opposite, no opposing force. It is the ultimate attitude adjuster and contains great power if used with conviction.

> "Holy smoke! We lost our last match and there's a storm coming!"
> Party On!
> "A flash flood swept away all our gear and we're twenty miles from the trail head!"
> Party On!
> "My femur bone's sticking through my skin and I've gotta cross that river!"
> Party On!

The hard core may wish to tattoo this statement on their foreheads, backwards, so it can be read in the mirror as a reminder.

The Essence of "Party On"

Most everyone is familiar with the plight of the Donner Party, a truly epic story. I highly recommend the documentary video *The Donner Party,* a PBS home video production that may be available at your local library. The Donner Party consisted of dozens of families traveling together with many women and children. Of the 88 people who began the 2,500-mile trek, 46 survived, two-thirds of whom were women and children.

On April 16, 1846, a caravan of nine covered wagons rolled out of Springfield, Illinois. It was the beginning of what would become a very cruel journey lasting several months on the Oregon Trail.

Months later, and less than 150 miles from their destination, the party missed crossing the Sierra Nevada Mountains by a few hours due to a snowstorm and were ultimately trapped by the worst winter on record. The weeks passed and the weather worsened. Their supplies dwindled, forcing most into eating the flesh of their dead comrades. The party sent out groups to locate help but most failed. Finally, after weeks trapped by many feet of snow, one of several rescue parties arrived. The going was rough and they could take only a few people out at a time while leaving virtually no supplies for the rest of the starving group. Those left behind had no choice but to wait until the party returned. In this case, due to the technology of the day, the waits involved several painful weeks, culminating in an overall rescue time of an unbelievable four months!

Through it all, one eight-year-old girl stands out amidst the carnage. Her name was Patty Reed. When the Donner Party trip began, her grandmother, who died less than two weeks out, had given her a little toy doll, which was her constant companion. Throughout her travels, Patty and the doll witnessed many hard times, including the banishment of her father for stabbing a man in self-defense during the heat of an argument. At this time morale was low and the group was unraveling fast as many had nearly died while crossing the Great Salt Lake desert.

Months later in the Sierra Nevada mountains of California, Patty passed up the opportunity to hike out with the first group of rescuers. One of her brothers, Thomas, was three years old and too small to walk in the deep snow. Patty opted instead to stay with him and told her distraught mother, who left with the first rescue party, "Well, ma, if you never see me again, do the best that you can." She stayed among the dead and dying, now apart from most of her family, for several more bitter cold weeks until she, too, finally walked out to freedom.

The documentary showed a picture of Patty decades later. She had lived to be an old woman, dying at the age of 93. The photograph shows her smiling broadly, proudly displaying the same little doll her grandmother had given her so many years before.

This story is the essence of "Party On." It is hard to imagine an ordeal you could get yourself into that would eclipse her experience. While others died all around her, she met challenge after challenge and succeeded, all at the tender young age of eight. Patty Reed's journey was and always will be a testament to the power of attitude.

Adaptation

Begin to cultivate an appreciation for doing more with less. Practice the ability to squeak out whatever you can from the resources presented to you. Traveling south of the border from my beloved state of Arizona, you'll come to a land where doing more with less isn't just a cute concept—it's a way of life. Many cash-poor communities in Mexico are used to improvising and adapting to their surroundings because they have to, while Americans head for the nearest discount store for a refund or exchange. The power of adaptation allows you to discover multiple uses for each item carried in your kit. It enables you to think like the critters that live in the very environment that threatens to take your life.

Animals are instinctual. They have little bias about meeting their needs by whatever means work. You cannot afford to be choosy when caught in a jam. In order to live, you have to recognize and exploit every resource and option available. Talking about survival scenarios is hypothetical at best, because each situation will be different and every person will react differently to his or her particular situation, adapting or not adapting. In addition, essential survival gear can be lost or damaged, requiring the former owner to improvise.

Awareness

You must become like the master adapter, the coyote, all senses alert for whatever might be of use. Without proper awareness, it's easy to walk by the water-filled cattle tank or miss the Jeep traveling the next ridge over. It's similar to walking down a seedy big-city street. If you insist on watching your feet instead of the road ahead with all its interesting characters, your chances of being mugged increase dramatically. Awareness also includes having the foresight to properly prepare for your journey. Pay attention to your surroundings! Your life may depend on this in the wilderness or the wilds of our cities.

REDUCING THE THREAT OF
THE SURVIVAL SITUATION:
THE SEVEN Ps

There's an old military saying called "the Seven Ps" that, if adhered to, can prevent many survival situations from occurring. The Seven Ps stand for *Proper Prior Planning Prevents Piss-Poor Performance.* They boil down to the ol' Boy Scout motto, "Be Prepared"! Careful planning is the foundation for creating a safer wilderness experience and is easily obtained in the information age in which we live. It involves taking the time to thoroughly research as many aspects as possible pertaining to your wilderness activity and destination, including current weather patterns, trail conditions, travel times, closures, fauna issues, detours, and so forth. Proper planning allows you to identify and understand potential dangers for your particular excursion and helps you develop a detailed equipment list, a healthy and realistic activity time line, alternate plans, and an emergency back-up plan(s).

At the very least, indigenous peoples living the world over always had with them some semblance of a survival kit. One of the reasons native peoples revered their elders was the fact that there were so damn few of them. To rely on nature to provide all of your needs all of the time is a gamble. Don't be fooled by instructors who perpetuate the myths that you can effortlessly "live off the fat of the land" or that survival is easy. Presenting information in such a fashion is extremely irresponsible, not to mention a lie, and produces arrogant, cocky students with little understanding of the power of nature and her infinite variables. There is a big difference between confident and cocky. The beauty of natural selection is that in time, it eventually weeds out the latter. A survival circumstance has a direct effect upon your life and

The Preparation Game: Check Off All Five for a Rewarding Backcountry Experience!

1. *Physical Preparation:* Outdoor activities are synonymous with physical stress and unique sanitary conditions. Maintaining a proper level of physical fitness, health, and hygiene is strongly recommended.
2. *Mental and Emotional Preparation:* Self-confidence is the key and is the result of proper prior planning, skills practice, personal belief systems, and your overall backcountry experience.
3. *Materials Preparation:* Pack the right equipment for the job (maintained and in proper working order) and know how to use it. Having back-up equipment for critical goods is wise in case of loss or failure.
4. *Dangerous Scenario Preparation:* Weird stuff happens. Play out possible nightmare scenarios with others in your party, including travel routes, leadership roles, and relevant environmental emergencies.
5. *Spiritual Preparation:* A strong grounding in a presence larger than oneself is an extremely powerful force and imparts the gift of a positive, holistic eagle's-eye view of the current situation and life in general. I have been fortunate enough to witness "atheists" praying during a compromised wilderness scenario, and it is a profound sight indeed.

Note: Outside of an ever-changing Mother Nature, the proverbial wild card lies in human nature and how it reacts to stress. Make every effort to get to know the other people in your tribe before crisis strikes.

those you love. It's not a game. Stack the deck in your favor using a complement of modern gear, common sense, humility, and good training.

WHAT IT TAKES TO STAY ALIVE: COMMON POWERFUL PERSONALITY PATTERNS FOR PEAK SURVIVOR PERFORMANCE

The following personality traits were found, at least in part, among those who have lived through life-threatening events. The list was compiled by folks who collect information on survivors. If you live through a life-threatening experience, they may want to interview you to see what you're made of. Keep in mind that these attributes make for a happier person in general, whether in the bush or the city. Ignoring these patterns could win you a spot on an altogether different list: the autopsy report.

Common personality traits of survivors

- The ability to keep calm and collected.
- The ability to improvise and adapt.
- The ability to make decisions.
- The ability to endure hardships.
- The ability to figure out the thoughts of others.
- The ability to hope for the best and prepare for the worst.
- The ability to maintain a sense of humor.

Calm and Collected

The ability to keep calm and collected sounds trite, but it is the foundation of a positive survival mind-set. It is the ability to prevent fear and panic from taking over your world, as both possess amazing powers to incapacitate body and mind. Prior training, whether physical, mental, or otherwise helps you deal more effectively with this ugly pair. It's physically necessary at times to STOP your body to allow greater clarity to surface.

STOP is a much-used acronym found in many survival books.

S = Stop
 T = Think
  O = Observe
   P = Plan
    A = Act!

The "S" stands for stop, which means to physically stop your body, sit down, and chill while attempting to lower your heart rate for greater mental and emotional clarity.

The "T" stands for think. Now that you have stopped your body, think about your situation.

The "O" stands for observe. While you sit thinking about your situation, observe all you can about your surroundings and the options you may have. Doing so allows the brain to analyze and identify threatening information gathered through the senses.

The "P" stands for plan. While you sit thinking about your situation and observing the possibilities, you start to form a plan.

Once the threat or threats have been assessed, the brain forms a strategy to deal with the issues at hand. This strategy will be affected by several factors, including prior training and practice, exposure to similar events in the past, fatigue, dehydration, and so forth. Once a plan has been developed, the brain shoots it off to the central nervous system to activate the required motor movements. Depending on your predicament, this process can happen in the blink of an eye or over a period of several hours or days.

The Swedish word for stop is *stopa*. Since a large part of my heritage is Swedish, I'll use the "A" and have it stand for act. No plan, no matter how well thought out, is worth beans unless it's acted upon.

Improvise and Adapt

The ability to improvise and adapt allows you to make use of every opportunity. It enables you to pack survival gear with more than one function, gear that allows for creating other gear. Traveling to any developing country imparts a profound respect and understanding of what can be done with limited resources. Most Americans have had it so good for so long, that their ability to adapt has become weak and flabby. They are slaves to the discount stores and their offerings of returns or cash-back guarantees. We rarely fix things anymore in America because we can return them.

Breathe Deep!

The power of breath control has been used for centuries by enlightened masters and warriors to accomplish everything from gaining greater clarity and calmness in the face of chaotic situations to controlling physical pain. Science is just starting to unearth the physiological proof that so many Americans seem to crave about why this is true. Unchecked fear and panic can easily lead to hyperventilation or, at the very least, anemic shallow breathing, which greatly impedes survival body resources and reaction times by elevating the heart rate, reducing oxygen to the cells, hindering concentration, and impairing the production of Adenosine Triphosphate (ATP), responsible for producing energy and heat. In fact, scientists have discovered that oxygen is the most vital component for the production of ATP, so breathe freely. In short, when the heart rate skyrockets due to increased stress, physical or otherwise, gaining control of breathing helps regain mental functions, motor skills, and energy production.

Simple Breathing Exercise

1. Inhale through your nose. The nose screens out harmful particulate matter from the air we breathe as well as warms excessively cold air. Nose breathing also boosts concentration.
2. Take a slow deep breath through your nose and into your belly, causing it to noticeably rise.
3. Breathe out through your nose or mouth, *emphasizing* and *lengthening* the exhalation, and repeat as necessary. The long exhalation, a phenomenon that occurs naturally when we sigh, helps activate the parasympathetic nervous system's relaxation response. Keep your awareness and concentration focused upon your breathing as you slowly inhale and exhale.
4. If you wish, count to three during your inhalation, hold the breath for three counts and then exhale for as long as is comfortable. If counting is distracting, blow it off and simply breathe slowly, fully, and rhythmically.

Make Decisions

The ability to make decisions allows you to thoroughly yet quickly formulate a game plan and then dutifully follow it through. I attended a college that has new students attend a thirty-day backpacking trip at the beginning of the school year. Four days after our group met, we were dropped off into the woods with instructors and seventy-plus-pound backpacks. The trip was grueling and involved miles of boulder hopping over knee-busting terrain. Before each meal we "group processed" about what we should eat. "Should we have spaghetti or falafel?" said one person. "Well, I don't know . . . falafel gives me gas," said another.

Meanwhile, back at my growling stomach, I prayed for a general consensus and a hot meal. Although we eventually ate, our tribe routinely burned thirty or more minutes each evening debating over food choices. In a life-threatening predicament, every decision is important.

Be decisive and take responsibility for your decisions. There's no room for passing-the-buck politics in the bush. Gather all the information possible about your surroundings and situation, formulate a plan, then do something about it! If plan "A" doesn't work, go to plan "B," and so on. Keep in mind that doing something about it might mean remaining where you are and conserving energy while awaiting rescue. Don't be afraid of failure and embarrassment by creating a game plan that doesn't work. You've already screwed up, or you wouldn't be in the situation—so what have you got to lose? Emergencies involving several people will need special finesse and leadership to obtain the intelligent discipline and organization required for success.

Endure Hardship

A survival situation is not comfortable. By its very nature it will tax you physically, mentally, emotionally, and spiritually. Your ability to endure hardship will be tested to its fullest extent. There are two great enemies to your survival and to life in general. One is the desire for comfort and the other is complacency. If this sounds like a summary of 90 percent of modern America, maybe it's just a coincidence. Desiring temporary comfort can spur you into making decisions that are irrational—all at the expense of a whim—and may be what propels you into a compromising situation in the first place. Comfort isn't bad, but there is a time and a place for it. You do want to make yourself as comfortable as possible during your episode, physically and otherwise, but don't weenie out and let a whim jeopardize your life. Training body

and mind far in advance of emergencies helps you deal with potential hardship. Realistic survival training cultivates a positive attitude and propels your mind into the land of "I know I can" instead of "I think I can."

Figure out the Thoughts of Others

Is the ability to figure out the thoughts of others some sort of psychic hotline thing? Think for a minute: How can intuition work to your advantage? Put yourself in your rescuers' shoes. Which direction will they come from? Where might they go first? What will they expect you to do as a survivor? Being sensitive to your surroundings includes the people in your party. Watch members of your group like a hawk for symptoms of fear, hypothermia, dehydration, and a host of other nasties. If your situation becomes long-term and resorts to cannibalism, having a good sense of intuition may come in handy around camp. Remember, what befalls one member of the tribe befalls all members of the tribe.

Hope for the Best and Prepare for the Worst

"The Ability to Hope for the Best and Prepare for the Worst" should be a bumper sticker, and somewhere it probably is. This is a heavy statement taking into account two major concepts. Hoping for the best is maintaining a positive attitude regardless of the seeming difficulties at hand. Preparing for the worst is just that: proper preparation. Get into the habit of doing both before any outdoor excursion.

Maintain a Sense of Humor

I have to admit that I added the ability to maintain a sense of humor. Humor is truly the grease between the gears, and has a great effect on human psychology and physiology.

I look to the Native Americans for a great example of this. Living in the Southwest, I'm frequently bombarded with tacky white-trash images of Native Americans. One of my least favorite images is the stoic guy riding the horse, slumped over and looking pretty whipped. The never-smiling face of this Hollywood Indian sports a streak from a small tear rolling down his face.

Several years ago I was given an informal Indian name, much to the delight of my Yavapai friends. It's Mayete (pronounced ma-yeh-tee). Can you guess what this means in Yavapai? It means "penis." My point is that the native people I know are constantly ribbing each other. Humor is very much a part of their lifestyle, far from the rigid stoicism sometimes pinned upon them from images like those I mentioned. Sure, all indigenous peoples were treated with astounding injustice for decades and many still are. But for most tribes, long before the coming of the white man, nature could be almost as callous. It's estimated that in the ancient Southwest one out of three babies died from disease and malnutrition before they were a year old. Fickle desert rainfall and drought made resources unpredictable causing tribal feuds, raiding, and warfare. And still the native person smiles. Many native people created special names for each other specifically to conjure up humor, such as "rat penis"—so much for the macho Indian names of the movies.

My point is this. As important as your body is to you, it's just a body. Do all you can to preserve the life within that's sacred, but don't forget to have some fun.

THE MOST COMMON WAY TO PUSH UP DAISIES IN THE OUTDOORS

The optimal ambient temperature in which humans are able to maintain body temperature without stress is 79° to 86°F (26° to 30°C). Statistically speaking, if you end up the loser in a survival situation, you'll die of exposure.

Exposure is a generic term for dying of *hypothermia* or *hyperthermia*. Mammals and birds are warm-blooded, or *homeothermic*, meaning they can maintain a relatively constant inner-body temperature, whereas other critters such as reptiles and attorneys are cold-blooded, or *poikilothermic*, meaning their body temperature varies according to the temperature of the environment.

In humans, core body temperature alternates in cycles throughout the day. While daily activity is responsible for some of this cycling, our body's circadian rhythm accounts for the majority. For the average person, inner temperatures are usually lowest in the early morning, around 97.9°F (36.6°C), with the late-afternoon high being approximately 99.3°F (37.3°C). Age is also an important factor, as some thermoregulatory responses are not fully developed until after puberty. Folks in their late sixties and older get screwed in three ways—from less sweating in reaction to heat, to reduced vasoconstrictor response and shivering in regard to combating the cold. Although body-temperature regulation between men and women is similar, several subtle differences in females are apparent, including a smaller blood volume, lower hemoglobin concentration, smaller lean body mass and heart, greater percentage of total body fat, greater surface-area-to-mass ratio, smaller shivering response, higher body-temperature set point for sweating, and geometrically thinner

98.6 Degrees: The Art of Keeping Your Ass Alive!

extremities. Females also have the added bonus of monthly temperature variation related to the menstrual cycle, pregnancy, and menopause.

Hypothermia

From the Greek *hypo* meaning "under", "beneath," or "below" and the Greek *therme* meaning "heat." Hypothermia is the dropping of your body's core temperature below 98.6°F (37°C). Controlled hypothermia is sometimes used in surgery to temporarily decrease a patient's metabolic rate. If your core temperature dips to 92°F (33°C) or less, you'll no longer be able to help yourself if you're traveling alone.

Hyperthermia

From the Greek *hyper* meaning "over," "above," or "excessive" and the Greek *therme* meaning "heat." Hyperthermia is the raising of your body's core temperature above 98.6°F (37°C). Anyone who has ever experienced a fever knows how wicked a few degrees above normal can feel. It was caused by a resetting of your temperature regulatory mechanism in response to fever-causing substances such as bacterial endotoxins or leucocyte extracts. At 107°F (41.6°C), the physical cells within your body literally begin to melt.

Fluctuation in core body temperature, high or low, of even a few degrees can severely compromise your ability to survive. To control its inner temperature, the body must be able to sense a change in environmental temperature and respond accordingly. To do so, the body is equipped with warm and cold receptors located in the skin, spinal cord, muscles, and brain that

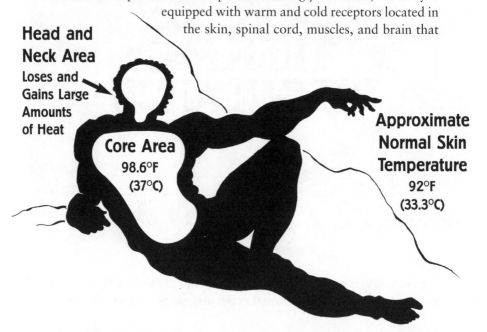

Head and Neck Area
Loses and Gains Large Amounts of Heat

Core Area
98.6°F
(37°C)

Approximate Normal Skin Temperature
92°F
(33.3°C)

begin physiological changes to quickly deal with outside extremes. Many variables contribute to the development and severity of hypothermia and hyperthermia, including a person's age, sex, health, nutrition, and body size; exhaustion; exposure; duration of exposure; wind; temperature; wetness; medications; intoxicants; and prior adaptation to heat or cold. Regulating core body temperature is called *thermoregulation* and is made possible by the wondrous physiological responses and reflexes called *vasoconstriction, vasodilation, shivering,* and *sweating.* Aside from basic physical necessities such as airway, breathing, and circulation, thermoregulating body temperature should be of prime importance in planning your next outdoor journey, regardless of its duration.

Temperature regulation in humans represents the balance between *heat production* from metabolic sources, such as digesting a corn dog, and *heat loss* from *respiration* and *evaporation* (sweating) and the physics of *radiation, convection,* and *conduction.* The metabolism of food to generate body heat is king, as decreases in core temperature elicit a metabolic response that is ten to twenty times greater than a similar reduction of skin temperature alone!

Once hypothermia develops, the heat deficit is shared by two body compartments: the shell and the core. Your outer skin, or "shell," consists of .065 inches of skin and has an average area of 2.2 square yards. This means that on an average, your shell accounts for only 10 percent of your total body mass. The rest of it is considered "the core." In other words, your body burns through calories like a madman when it senses a drop in core temperature.

Temperature regulatory mechanisms act through the autonomic nervous system and are largely controlled by the hypothalamus. The big "H" responds to stimuli from nerve receptors in your skin, the largest organ in the body.

When It's Cold

In a cold environment, body heat is conserved first by the constriction of blood vessels near the body's surface (vasoconstriction), keeping the majority of blood (heat) in the core. Doing so allows the body to use the skin and underlying fatty layer as insulation.

The one area of skin that doesn't constrict blood flow is the scalp, which remains at a fairly constant temperature regardless of outside extremes. This is one reason why the head (and neck) loses and gains heat like crazy. In its attempt to regulate temperature, the body is a master at changing blood flow to the skin. With blood vessels dilated wide open in hot weather, it can circulate in the skin alone more than four quarts of blood every minute. In cold weather, blood vessels constrict skin blood flow to an amazing 99 percent of the former, a mere 0.02 quarts per minute! Ironically, when temperatures continue to drop, blood vessels in the skin dilate (vasodilation) and, if temperatures drop further, alternate back and forth between dilation and constriction in the body's attempt to ensure that the skin remains undamaged from the cold. The result is your red nose, ears, hands, and other appendages in the wintertime. If outside temperatures continue to plummet, however, surface blood vessels constrict continuously.

Chillin' Out: A World Record

The dubious honor for the world's lowest recorded body temperature in an adult, with ultimate survival, goes to an anonymous 23-year-old homeless woman found sleeping on the streets of Chicago. The outside air temperature at the time was −11°F (−24°C). Although she was thought to be dead upon arrival at the hospital, doctors discovered that her heart was still slowly beating. Her core temperature was an unbelievable 64°F (18°C)!

Second in the body's response to cold is uncoordinated waves of muscle contractions, more commonly referred to as shivering. Shivering utilizes small parts of the skeletal muscles called motor units that contract around 10 to 20 times per second and can increase your metabolism fivefold! The energy needed for shivering comes from fats and simple sugars (carbohydrates) and can be used up quickly unless you consume additional food. Shivering decreases when carbon dioxide levels raise (a poorly ventilated shelter) or when the oxygen in the air becomes thinner (extremes in altitude), and through the use of alcohol, which impairs the shivering response. Since blood vessels are essentially the pipes your body uses to heat itself by forcing warmed blood throughout the body, ingesting substances that dilate surface blood vessels is a dumb move. Purposely constricting blood vessels is also a bad move, whether through nicotine use, dehydration, or another means. Dehydration slowly turns your blood into ketchup, making it that much harder for the heart to circulate the sludge around the body in order to keep inner temperatures stable. Low temperatures also change the composition of blood, making it thicker by up to 21 percent, by increasing the number of particles, such as platelets, red blood cells, and cholesterol. Another heat-conserving feature most impressive in Bigfoot and other really hairy folks is goose bumps, or *piloerection*. Goose bumps raise body hairs, thereby creating tiny air pockets of insulation.

In time, your metabolism speeds up, burning extra calories in order to produce more heat. But the body has only so many tricks up its sleeve

98.6 Degrees: The Art of Keeping Your Ass Alive!

without outside help. Regardless of how many candy bars you can cram into your mouth, when outside temperatures drop and you're stuck with limited clothing, you won't be able to sufficiently increase your metabolic rate to replace the heat you'll lose to the environment.

When It's Hot

There are approximately 400 environmental heat-related deaths every year in the United States, with thousands more occurring during heat waves, droughts, and increased illegal immigration in the Southwest. When it's hot outside, heat must be lost to maintain body temperature. Increased surface blood flow through dilated vessels, especially in the arms and legs, works at dissipating extra heat by exploiting the major surface areas of the body as well as avoiding the insulating properties of subcutaneous fat. Again, if you allow your blood to turn to ketchup through dehydration, this activity is severely compromised. This, cou-

A Cold-Blooded Killer

Humans are amazingly poor in their ability to physiologically adapt to cold environments. The brutal effects of cold weather and the toll they take on human life are legendary and are responsible for decimating countless armies throughout history. Alexander the Great was knocked off by hypothermia, as well as countless Roman legionnaires in the high country. In his attack on Russia, Napoleon's once proud, 500,000-man army, through the combined insults of combat and cold, were reduced to about 40,000 men. Many who survived did so by killing their horses and crawling inside the warm carcasses while others, desperately hungry from the cold, pillaged local medical schools to eat preserved human organs. In World War I, cold-weather deaths for combined British, French, and Italian forces were estimated as high as 233,000 individuals. Even in the face of such amazing statistics, bear in mind that the majority of deaths from hypothermia happen when air temperatures are between 30°F (–1°C) and 50°F (10°C).

SIGNS AND SYMPTOMS OF:

HYPOTHERMIA

HYPERTHERMIA

Early Signs and Symptoms
[core temperature 95°F (35°C) to 96°F (35.5°C)]

- Shivering
- Decreased awareness
- Unable to think or solve problems
- Apathy
- Confusion
- Skin pale and cool to the touch
- Numbness (stinging pain)
- Loss of dexterity
- Deterioration of fine and complex motor skills

Advancing Signs and Symptoms
[core temperature 93°F (33.8°C) to 94°F (34.4°C)]

- Obvious shivering
- Stumbling
- Little or no effort to protect oneself
- Unaware of present situation

Advanced Signs and Symptoms
[core temperature 91°F (32.7°C) to 92°F (33.3°C)]

- Intense shivering
- Difficulty walking
- Thick or slurred speech
- No effort to protect oneself
- Skin appears ashen gray and cold
- Possible hallucinations

The Death Zone
[core temperature 87°F (30.5°C) to 90°F (32.2°C)]

- Shivering comes in waves
- Unable to walk
- Speech very difficult to understand

If the core temperature continues to drop, shivering will cease, breathing and pulse will appear absent, and the skin will become blue in color. Death quickly follows.

If elevated core temperatures remain constant or continue to rise, death will rear its ugly head.

Signs and Symptoms of Heat Stroke [core temperature 103°F (39.4°C) to 106°F (41.1°C)]

- Disorientation and confusion
- Hot, flushed, potentially dry skin (classic heat stroke) or hot, flushed, sweaty skin (exertional heat stroke)
- Elevated body temperature
- Rapid, bounding pulse or rapid, weak pulse
- Initial deep breathing, rapidly progressing to shallow breathing, followed by absence of breath
- Dilated, sluggish pupils
- Delirium
- Little or no effort to protect oneself
- Unaware of present situation
- Seizures
- Stroke
- Coma

Signs and Symptoms of Heat Exhaustion [core temperature 101°F (38.3°C) to 102°F (38.8°C)]

- Excessive thirst
- Profuse sweating
- Headache
- Dizziness
- Nausea, vomiting
- Generalized weakness, decreased appetite
- Disorientation and confusion
- Cramps
- Weak, rapid pulse with shallow, rapid breathing
- Cool, pale, moist skin
- Decreased awareness or unconsciousness

Signs and Symptoms of Heat Cramps [core temperature 99°F (37.2°C) to 100°F (37.7°C)]

- Thirst
- Profuse sweating
- Headache and dizziness
- Nausea, vomiting
- Generalized weakness
- Spasms of the voluntary muscles and abdomen after exercise and exertion in a hot environment
- Deterioration of fine and complex motor skills

98.6 Degrees: The Art of Keeping Your Ass Alive!

pled with the wonders of evaporative heat loss through increased sweating, is the main tool your body uses to stabilize its inner core when environmental temperatures climb.

Charts and graphs in books bore me silly. That said, if I didn't include a signs-and-symptoms chart for hypothermia and hyperthermia I'd be a doo-doo head. A *sign* is a condition(s) you see in someone else while a *symptom* is a condition(s) you tell someone else. While looking at the illustration on the opposite page, note that the psychological signs and symptoms of hypothermia and hyperthermia are very similar, involving disorientation and poor coordination. These similarities are no accident and offer vital clues into a person's physiology. *Being able to recognize the signs and symptoms of exposure in yourself and others is mandatory, as these are the body's warning signs that things are getting out of whack on a cellular level.* The majority of people who die from exposure have ample early warnings that they flat out ignored. These signs are your second chance to circle the wagons and manipulate your environment in whatever way you can to prevent heat loss or gain and the sooner the better. Ignore the signs, especially those occurring from the onset, and you might feed worms. Keep in mind that the signs and symptoms shown include only behaviors that can be readily understood in the field using no medical gear.

Signs and Symptoms of Hyperthermia

There are three levels of environmental heat illness recognized throughout the medical profession. Listed in the order of their severity—from "hey, let's rest in the shade and cool down a bit" to "why is Uncle Frank curling up in the fetal position while in a coma?"—they are *heat cramps, heat exhaustion,* and *heat stroke.* There are two types of heat stroke, *classical heat stroke* and *exertional heat stroke.* Classical heat stroke generally occurs in sedentary older folks who decide to mow the lawn at noon in July. Exertional heat stroke happens after intense physical activity in a hot environment, especially during periods of high humidity, which prevents the cooling power of evaporation. During this type of heat stroke, despite earlier beliefs, the victim may still be sweating heavily as the sweat glands are usually still active at the time of collapse. As suggested, heat stroke is one bad dude and should be avoided at all costs by paying attention to the signs and symptoms of heat cramps.

How to Screw Up a Cell Membrane

Biochemicals are molecules constructed by a living system. Living systems are composed of large units, such as organs, muscles, and bones, and small units, such as cells that form the large ones. The human body is composed of around 50 billion cells, all of which contain water, among other goodies, and change viscosity, pH, and electrostatic charge. Even smaller units called *organelles* lie within the cells themselves and come neatly packaged. Cell membranes or "walls" are permeable and consist of lipids or fats—saturated fats to be exact—and are stacked like shelves holding all sorts of life-giving matter. Through these wall-like membranes, cells make and break bonds at precise rates, such as our sodium and potassium balance. The membranes, being made of fat, are very sensitive to changes in temperature.

When the body's temperature drops, proteins within the cells start to clump, creating holes, while water in and around the cells freeze to form jagged ice crystals that shred the delicate membranes. When the thermometer rises, cell membranes begin to lose their elasticity and can actually melt. With cell membranes frazzled, precision rates are altered and once-pristine body systems fall into a state of unregulated pandemonium. **Fluctuations in core body temperature literally cause chaos on a cellular level, chaos you can see in the uncoordinated signs and symptoms of hypothermia and hyperthermia.**

HOW YOUR BODY LOSES AND GAINS HEAT: THE PHYSICS OF FREEZING YOUR FANNY OR BAKING YOUR BONES

*H*ere on Earth, your body loses and gains heat through several physical laws described below. Unless you've progressed enough spiritually to tap into higher realms, all life, to a greater or lesser extent, is bound by these laws. By recognizing the general physics involved in heat loss and gain, the survivor can intelligently assess virtually any situation placed before them and deal with the problems one by one. Don't freak out on the big words; just understand the simple principles behind them. Life, after all, is very simple—we choose to make it complex because it's better for the economy.

Conduction

Conduction is the transfer of heat through direct contact with an object, including hot or cold air against the skin. The direction of heat flow is always from a warmer to a cooler temperature. Anytime you touch something that's less than 92°F (33°C) (your approximate normal skin temperature), you lose heat through conduction. If the object touched is warmer than 92°F (33°C), your body gains heat. Substances vary in their thermal conductivity quite radically. Water has twenty-five times the conductivity of air, while muscles possess nearly twice the tissue conductivity of fat. Unless you find yourself frequently floating, feet or other parts of the anatomy are in constant contact with the ground, hence the need for insulation in hot *and* cold environments. Hot desert ground temperatures can become almost unbearable. One summer, while "reconning" for a desert survival course, I completely delaminated the soles from a new pair of sandals in less than thirty minutes! Under normal conditions, conduction accounts for approximately 2 percent of the body's heat loss for a standing person.

Convection

Convection is the transfer of heat through currents in air and liquids and can be either forced or natural. An example of forced convection would be rolling down the windows of a moving car or sitting in front of a fan. Natural convection happens when density changes in heating or cooling molecules next to the body cause them to move away from the body itself. We all possess a boundary layer of slower moving molecules directly against our skin that is produced by the body's radiant heat. This layer, which is only a few millimeters thick, equals a constant three-mile-per-hour wind. For example, anyone who climbs into a scalding hot tub will do so very slowly and with much grimacing. After sitting still for a few minutes, however, the heat doesn't seem to be nearly as potent . . . until some dimwit bumps you and disturbs your boundary layer. All of a sudden, the water miraculously seems a lot hotter.

Classic convection experienced by every outdoor traveler is the wind. "Wind chill," a term coined by American explorer Paul Siple, causes existing outside air temperatures to feel a heck of a lot colder than they actually are and is a common killer of all outdoor enthusiasts, as it greatly increases the possibility of death through hypothermia. In contrast, hot desert winds can feel like a hair dryer on the skin. They suck away evaporating sweat so quickly that you might not think it's hot because it appears as if you're not sweating. Sweat evaporating from the skin at such an accelerated rate does little to help cool the body. According to paleoanthropologists, the oldest structure ever found is a windbreak built by early hominids in Africa more than 3.25 million years ago, proving that protection from the wind has been in vogue for a very long time.

Convection features almost as many variables as there are corporate tax breaks, including surface shape, density, surface temperature profiles, flow dynamics, conductivity, and specific heat. This crazy variation means that convective heat loss or gain is a wilderness wild card that can cause you to push up daisies. Researchers have found that under neutral conditions, 40 percent of the heat loss from a naked human body stems from convection—add wet clothing and/or strong winds to the scenario, which are common occurrences in the outdoors, and the percentage climbs drastically.

Radiation

Radiation is the act of losing or gaining heat through radiation. There are two types of radiation we're concerned with. Terrestrial, or *long-wave* radiation, emanates from fire, a human body, or just about anything else on the planet having a temperature greater than absolute zero or −460°F (−273°C). Radiated body heat is the emission of electromagnetic energy in infrared wavelengths of which the body is both emitting and receiving. Curling up in the fetal position reduces your radiant heat loss by 35 percent, compared to a person standing with arms away from their sides. Snuggling next to your honey on a cold winter night means you're enjoying his or her long-wave radiation, which for mammals is somewhat constant. Creativity with this concept can result in a grab bag of fresh pick-up lines at the neighborhood bar. Radiant heat loss is a force to be reckoned with, as it accounts for around 45 percent of the total heat loss from a nude body in neutral conditions. Surfaces that are good at absorbing radiation are also good at emitting it.

Short-wave radiation emanates from the sun and varies in its intensity according to the time of day, altitude, latitude, surface reflection, atmospheric pollution, ozone levels, and season. Most ultraviolet radiation bathes the Earth at mid-day, 80 percent between the hours of 9 A.M. and 3 P.M. and 65 percent between 10 A.M. and 2 P.M. Radiation from sunlight can heat a person in three ways: directly on the skin, reflected off particulate matter in the atmosphere, and reflected off the ground. Unlike long-wave radiation, short-wave radiation is absorbed to a greater extent by darker colored clothing and skin pigmentation. In hot climates, all can lead to dehydration and hyperthermia if not properly managed.

Evaporation

Evaporation is the act of losing heat through the conversion of a liquid to a gas. The principal way your body loses heat in a hot environment is the evaporation of water in the form of sweat upon your skin, as well as a small amount of evaporative cooling gained from exhaled moisture. A gram of sweat evaporating off skin with a normal temperature loses about 580 calories of heat. In the desert during July, the 2.6 million sweat glands humans have act as a savior. On the other hand,

How Your Body Gains Heat

Benny the Bum

<u>Body Type:</u> Larger surface area to volume ratio superior at eliminating excess heat

A: Direct Solar Gain (Radiation).

B: Breathing Through Nose Limits Water Loss (Respiration).

C: Hot Wind (Convection).

D: Reflected Particulate Matter Solar Gain (Radiation).

E: Nicotine: Diuretic, Constricts Blood Vessels, Increases BMR.

F: Insulation from Hot Ground (Conduction).

G: Ground Reflected Solar Gain (Radiation).

H: Alcohol: Diuretic, Impaired Judgment, Increased Blood Viscosity.

Benny the Bum loses heat through:

I: Increased Heat Loss Through Wet Clothing (Evaporation).

How Your Body Loses Heat

Homeless Hal

Body Type: Larger volume to surface area ratio superior at minimizing heat loss

A: Cold Wind (Convection).

B: Alcohol: Diuretic, Impaired Judgment, Increased Blood Flow to Skin.

C: Increased Heat Loss Through Wet Clothing (Evaporation).

D: Insulation from Cold Ground (Conduction).

E: Reduced Insolation (Incoming Solar Radiation).

F: Water Loss Through Breath (Respiration).

Homeless Hal gains heat through:

G: Food (Metabolic Heat).

H: Fire (Radiation).

in the winter cold, clothing that is sweaty from over-exertion will place you one step closer to death by increasing your chance of hypothermia. Interestingly enough, most mammals don't have sweat glands but keep cool by panting (evaporation through the respiratory tract), increased salivation, and skin and fur licking.

Respiration

Respiration is the act of losing heat and water vapor through the respiratory surfaces of the lungs by breathing. The air you inhale must be humidified by the body to saturation in order to be used efficiently. When this vapor is exhaled, the resulting evaporative heat loss at high altitudes can rival sweat as a cooling factor. More typically, however, respiration heat loss is minor in comparison to the others previously mentioned. A tremendous amount of water can be lost through the breath, especially in extremely cold temperatures. Cold, dry air breathed into warm, moist lungs pulls out as much as two quarts of water daily in –40°F (–40°C) temperatures. In some instances, the same condition can destroy the cells lining the respiratory tract.

Cold Temperatures

In summary, walking around in cold temperatures without insulated footwear or lying on noninsulated ground (conduction) while wearing sweaty cotton clothing (evaporation) in the wind (convection) without the ability to make a fire (radiation) can kill you.

Hot Temperatures

In hot temperatures, radiation from the sun (times three) directly on the skin, reflected off the ground, and reflected off particulate matter in the air, can heat up conductive ground surfaces in excess of 150°F (66°C). This helps produce heated convective winds capable of evaporating sweat obscenely fast with little cooling effect for the body. Add the crushing effect of metabolic heat produced by trying to dig the car out of a wash at noon, and you have a serious set-up for dehydration, hyperthermia, and death.

The Cold-Weather Bottom Line

1. *Produce heat.*
   Exercise using the body's larger muscle groups (squats); eat calorie-dense foods, especially carbohydrates, frequently throughout the day; create fire in conjunction with space blankets or other reflectors if possible; locate south-facing microclimates for maximal sun exposure; hydrate using warm/hot fluids with dissolved hard candy or other sugars when available.

2. *Decrease heat loss.*
   Wear proper clothing especially in the head, neck, and torso areas; replace wet clothing with dry; create or find shelter from the elements; decrease surface area while increasing volume; avoid or insulate the body from cold surfaces.

3. *Avoid becoming exhausted (60 percent rule).*
   Working at 60 percent allows the body to burn fat reserves instead of using up glucose and glycogen stores. Get adequate sleep and rest.

4. *Reduce internal and external constriction.*
   Avoid ingesting vasoconstricting substances; tight clothing, equipment, and footwear.

5. *Stay hydrated.*
   Drink warm to hot liquids if possible; urine should appear "clear."

6. *Stay aware of what's happening.*
   Be conservative. Don't take unnecessary chances. Cultivate and maintain a "Party On" attitude.

Once you are familiar with how your body loses and gains heat, it's easy to understand how an innocent little day hike, through the compounded result of basic physics, can turn into a life-threatening state of affairs. In the case of lost or forgotten gear, learning the basics of heat transfer allows you to improvise insulation and other needs directly from the wilderness.

The Hot-Weather Bottom Line

1. *Reduce heat gain.*

   Stay in the shade; create or find shelter with air movement; insulate the body and avoid hot surfaces by going above or below scorching ground temperatures if possible; seek cooler north-facing microclimates with minimal sun exposure; avoid physical exertion during the afternoon; wear proper clothing; keep hydrated; save movement for early morning, late evening, or night.

2. *Increase heat loss.*

   Increase surface area while decreasing volume; wet clothing if possible, especially the head, neck, trunk, and groin areas; increase air movement; lie on or against cooler microclimates.

3. *Avoid becoming exhausted (60 percent rule).*

   Working at 60 percent allows the body to burn fat reserves instead of using up glucose and glycogen stores; rest and conserve during afternoon heat. Get adequate sleep.

4. *Reduce internal and external constriction.*

   Avoid ingesting vasoconstricting substances; tight clothing, equipment, and footwear.

5. *Stay hydrated.*

   Drink cool to cold liquids if possible; urine should appear "clear"; shut mouth and breathe through the nose; limit talking.

6. *Stay aware of what's happening.*

   Be conservative. Don't take unnecessary chances. Cultivate and maintain a "Party On" attitude.

10

YOUR FIRST LINE OF DEFENSE

Statistically speaking, your first line of defense is to regulate core body temperature. In one of my lectures, I have students define their *needs* from their *wants*. The situation is this. You've been invited to Fantasy Island to achieve your lifelong dream of the ultimate camping trip. Tattoo and Mr. Rourke beckon you to enter the island's mega-camping store. Inside, you find all the outdoor gear your heart could desire. Gear galore waits in every corner—it's expensive, shiny, and it's all free as Rourke is footing the bill. Using this image, my students brainstorm every piece of camping gear imaginable as I write furiously on the blackboard to keep up. These are the wants. All good Americans worth their credit cards know the world is full of wants. Very few are truly aware that they will never be satisfied.

I then propose the scenario of regulating body temperature. What from the list of wants would they need to regulate core body temperature? I don't give a specific situation or agenda. The time you're not going to find yourself in a compromising dilemma is when you plan on being in one. You won't have just consumed a big bowl of cereal after ten hours of beauty rest.

"Survival situation? Hmmm, let me check my day planner. Oh yes, I have an opening at three next Tuesday."

You won't be able to choose your emergency. It's just gonna happen! That's part of what makes it a survival situation. So, I ask my students, what do they need to regulate body temperature? Out of the massive list on the blackboard, past the toaster oven, the bicycle, and the RV, appear two simple, sacred items: *clothing* and *water*.

Your body generates 300 BTUs of heat every hour. A BTU is a British Thermal Unit, the amount of heat it takes to bring one pint (or pound) of water up 1°F (bring 453.6 grams of water up 0.56°C; about 1.06 kiloJoules). So who cares? One strike-anywhere kitchen match burned completely through is a BTU. There are 250 strike-anywhere kitchen matches per box. Your body generates the equivalent heat of over a box of wooden kitchen matches every hour! That's a lot of heat.

Cold Weather

In a cold-weather situation, the simplest means of staying warm is to trap this heat using insulation or dead air space in the form of clothing, adding or subtracting layers as outdoor conditions warrant. In addition, physical exercise, fire craft, shelter, and calorie-rich foods all help to keep the survivor's core temperature at a lively 98.6°F (37°C). Even mild cold affects the body by impairing nerve functions, decreasing sensation, and reducing manual dexterity. Cold muscles work slower and with less efficiency, which greatly retards the ability to perform seemingly simple tasks—another plug for packing gear with limited bells and whistles. While there are variations, the critical temperature for retaining manual dexterity is a balmy 54°F (12°C) while touch sensitivity is 46°F (8°C).

Hot Weather

Alternately, there is a reason the Bedouin nomads in the Middle East wear long, flowing woolen robes in extreme desert temperatures. Your skin is the largest organ of the body. Burn it, and you severely compromise your body's ability to cool itself, as even a moderate sunburn causes a decrease in the responsiveness and capacity of the sweat glands. Chemical sunscreens were discovered in 1926 and sold to the general public in 1928. Long before this, southwestern people used alternatives such as prickly-pear cactus slime and carbon from a spent fire. Carbon, the black stuff leftover after putting out a fire, works especially well as a total sun block when finely ground and rubbed onto the skin. Clothing protects your skin from direct solar radiation as well as radiation reflected off particles in the atmosphere and the ground. Ground reflection can be major and varies from 2.5 percent for grass, to 20 percent for sand, and on up to 100 percent for certain bodies of water. The most important factor in determining how a fabric will repel ultraviolet radiation is the tightness of its weave followed by its color and if the fabric is wet or dry. Specialized, sun-protective clothing is becoming more common and, in the United States, is actually regulated as a medical device. Manufacturers have various strategies to keep out the sun's rays, including tightly woven nylon, chemically treated cotton, cotton/synthetic blends, clothing bonded with ultraviolet-radiation-absorbing devices, and chemical shields added to laundry detergents. In short, clothing helps prevent sunburn.

98.6 Degrees: The Art of Keeping Your Ass Alive!

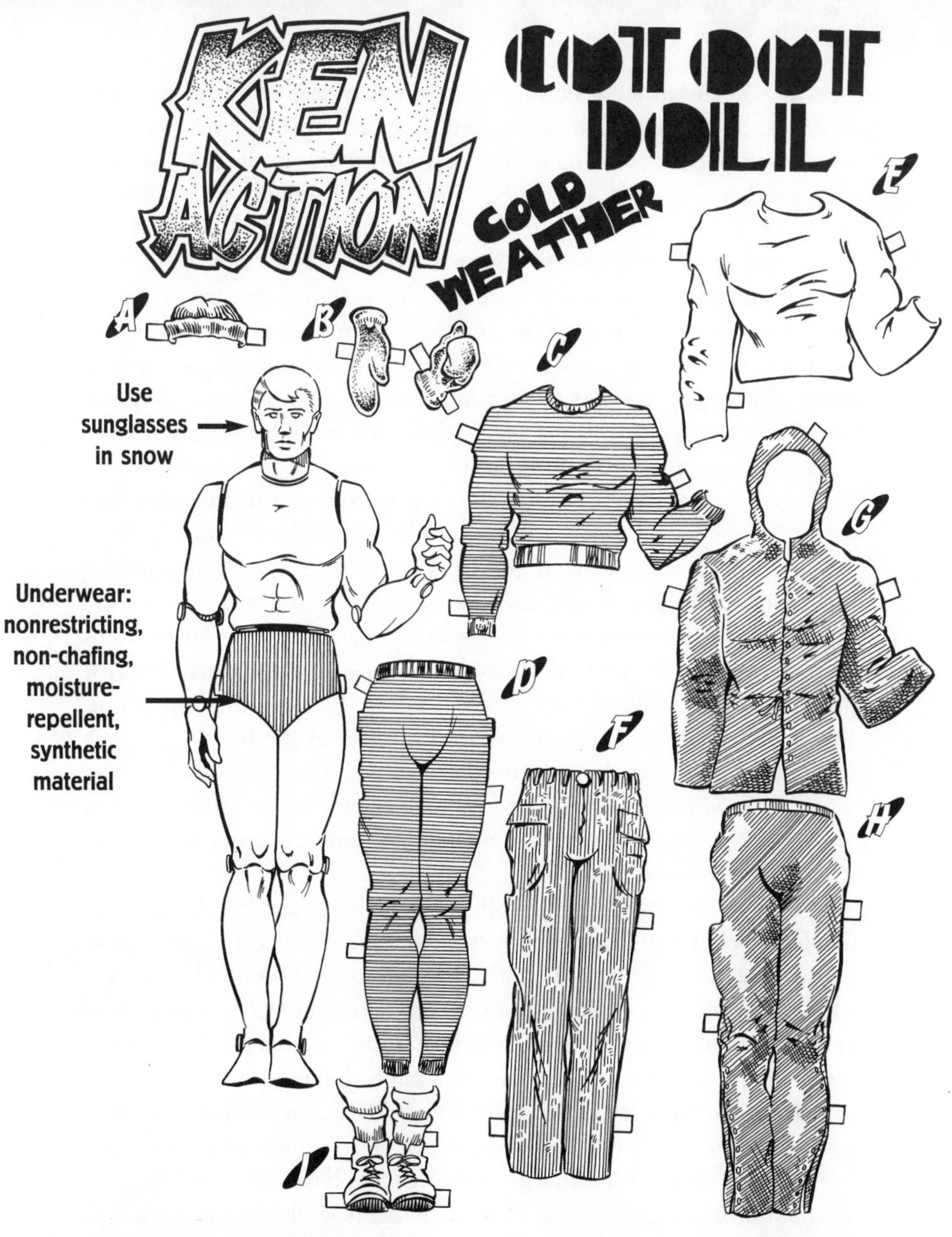

KEN ACTION

CUT OUT DOLL

COLD WEATHER

A

B

C

E

G

D

F

H

Use sunglasses → in snow

Underwear: nonrestricting, non-chafing, moisture-repellent, synthetic material

I

A: Brightly colored, loose-fitting, insulating, wind-resistant wool or synthetic material.

B: Nonrestricting, insulating wool or synthetic material.

C and D: Base Layers: Dark-colored, moisture-wicking, nonirritating, formfitting yet non-restricting wool, silk or polypropelene material. Avoid cotton!

E and F: Insulation Layers: Light- or dark-colored, nonrestricting, easy-on-and-off, ventable, easy-packing, resistant-to-moisture-accumulation wool or synthetic material. Add and subtract layers as needed.

G and H: Environmental Layers: Bright- or dark-colored, light-weight, loose-fitting, ventable, wind- and water-resistant, abrasion-resistant, synthetic-material shell.

I: Insulating, formfitting yet nonconstricting wool or synthetic socks. Avoid cotton! Well-fitted, broken-in, water-resistant, insulated boots.

In a hot-weather situation, when ambient temperatures are near or above body temperatures, limiting heat loss through vasodilation, your body relies on one main mechanism to cool itself. This involves the sacred substance called water, entering your mouth and ending up in the large intestine where it's absorbed and circulated through the body, and, when necessary, deposited on the skin in the form of sweat. This wonderful, liquid nectar, which is 99 percent water with a pinch of sodium chloride (salt) and potassium, is the only way your body cools itself when subjected to elevated temperatures. Even at a paltry 1 percent, long-term sweating without the ability to consume salt poses serious problems. People acclimated to hot weather produce more sweat, but with a lower concentration of lost salts.

Sweat glands are found in the skin in concentrations from 650 to 4,000 per square inch and occur most abundantly on the forehead, scalp, face, neck, front and back portions of the trunk, and the top of the hands and forearms. The face and scalp alone account for an incredible 50 percent of the body's total sweat production! In fact, the only skin areas that don't have sweat glands are the lips, nipples, and external genitals. Sweat cools the skin and, the blood flowing through it. The cooled blood returns to the body's core via the veins where it picks up more heated blood and returns it to the skin's surface for cooling. Any liquid that evaporates from the skin will work, so don't be shy about peeing on your clothing or soaking it in scummy water.

Every drop of sweat that rolls off your body and hits the ground has been wasted. It has been wasted because it failed to accomplish its purpose by cooling your body through evaporation. The conversion of a liquid to a vapor requires a certain amount of energy or heat called the *heat of vaporization* and is directly responsible for wicking away the high temperatures that threaten to bake your brain.

High humidity levels, especially those 70 percent or higher, severely restrict the evaporation process. Regardless of how much water you have available, if your body can't get rid of excess heat, you risk dying of dehydration and hyperthermia. Personal humidity levels close to the body's surface may skyrocket if you wear poorly ventilated clothing, as it reduces airflow over the skin. High water-vapor pressure, a.k.a. humidity, causes sweat to simply drip off the skin instead of evaporate. Many folks in humid environments commonly experience taking a shower, drying off, then drying off, and then trying to dry off again. High temperatures combined with high humidity levels can kill and are responsible for summer heatwaves in eastern North America that wipe out hundreds of people.

98.6 Degrees: The Art of Keeping Your Ass Alive!

Willy Nilly DESERT CLOTHING CUT-OUT Doll

Upturned collar to protect neck

Oversized sleeves rolled down to protect back of hands

Underwear: loose fitting, non-chafing cotton material (hearts optional)

A: Sunglasses for protection against UV radiation and blowing particulate matter.

B: Wide-brimmed, light-colored, breathable hat with light-colored, cotton-bandana neck protection.

C: Base Layer: Fairly new, loose-fitting, light-colored cotton T-shirt.

D: Insulation / Environmental Layer(s): Oversized, light-colored, long-sleeved, abrasion-resistant, cotton material. Add and subtract layers as needed.

E: Environmental Layer: Loose-fitting, non-chafing, light-colored, abrasion-resistant, cotton material.

F: Insulating, formfitting yet nonrestricting wool or synthetic socks. Avoid cotton! Well-fitted, broken in, insulated, lightweight boots.

Not only does clothing insulate you from heat and cold, it allows the sweat upon your skin to evaporate slowly and efficiently, making maximal use of whatever water you already have. With cotton, the same hydrophilic properties that kill you in a winter scenario make cotton a wonderful choice in desert heat. Believe it or not, I know folks who feel the same way about wool. The trick is to find out what works best for you in hot and cold weather.

The Layering System

Using the layering system, clothing for both hot and cold environments can be categorized into the following three sections: *base layers, insulation layers,* and *environmental layers.* Base layers are used against the skin, trapping air close to the body. They should be made from a fabric that insulates while transporting (wicking) water vapor away from the body and should be nonirritating and nonconstricting. Insulation layers are added or subtracted between the base and environmental layers as outside temperatures warrant. Environmental layers protect against outdoor elements such as wind, rain, snow, sun, and brush, and should be lightweight, durable, loose fitting, wind- and water-resistant, and easy to vent excess moisture buildup. "Water-resistant" and "waterproof" are two entirely different concepts. The former "breathes" to a certain extent to let body moisture escape, and the latter is a vapor barrier that, although useful in some applications, requires advanced thought and the right conditions to be used successfully. Telling the difference between the two fabrics is easy by blowing on the fabric in question from the inside out and feeling for your escaping breath on the other side. If you feel warm air, it's water-resistant material. Waterproofing and breathability are the oil and water components most coveted by outdoor enthusiasts in an environmental layer. Unfortunately, if you work at an intensity greater than 50 percent of your maximum oxygen uptake, a level of activity that a physically fit person can continue for hours, no fabric on the market can do ideal justice to both concepts.

Dressing for extremely cold, sub-zero weather is an art form and beyond the scope of this book in regard to particular gear recommendations. Nevertheless, all clothing systems for any climate involve dead-air space or insulation. Your experience and ability to adjust your particular clothing system is more dependable than specialized gear. Clothing insulation is measured in *clo.* Technically speaking, one clo is equivalent to the amount of insulation needed to keep a seated person comfy in an air temperature of 70°F (21°C), with a relative humidity of less than 50 percent, and air movement of .2 miles per hour. To make

98.6 Degrees: The Art of Keeping Your Ass Alive!

things simpler, a common business suit provides one clo's worth of insulation. Insulation is much more effective when worn in several thin layers as opposed to one thick layer, as it allows you to not only adapt to changing temperatures, but the air space between the layers of clothing insulates as well while adding no weight, bulk, or cost to the user. The layers should increase in size so as not to constrict the body when worn on top of one another. They should also be easy to pack, easy to put on and take off, and resist moisture accumulation. The best insulation has spaces small enough to prevent convective air currents, ideally no bigger than a millimeter, and should be able to trap air molecules through electrostatic attraction. Insulation types vary according to weight, compressibility, moisture repellence, and cost.

> *The ideal scenario in the **cold** is to regulate clothing layers and activities to allow you to operate at peak performances without wasting water and energy to sweating or shivering.*

For most outdoor recreationists, clothing decisions are based upon factors of cost, weight, bulk, fit, material properties, environmental temperature, and unfortunately, fashion. For all general purposes, your clothing needs to keep you warm, cool, out of the sun, away from bugs, and to be quick drying, durable, and nonrestrictive. What clothing you choose to pack is largely determined by the length of your trip and what climate and season you're headed for. The layering method allows you to add or subtract layers of clothing at will in response to your increasing or decreasing metabolic output and the environmental temperatures at hand. This ability to fine-tune your wardrobe helps minimize sweating in your clothes. "Running cool" by wearing slightly less clothing than required, providing there's no need to conserve energy, is an effective way to prevent sweating. In cold temperatures, sweated-out clothing through over-exertion severely compromises your clothing's ability to insulate. Regardless of physical activity, the skin continually pours out moisture called *insensible perspiration.* When this or any warmed water vapor reaches cold air, it freezes. Insulation filled with frost and water does little to keep you alive; thus venting excess moisture in cold conditions is of paramount importance. The advantages of not sweating are many, including the fact that the insulation layers stay drier and warmer when activity ceases; clothes remain cleaner longer; and you achieve a lower metabolic rate, which conserves precious energy and water. The ideal scenario in the cold is to regulate

> *The ideal scenario in the heat is to regulate layers and physical activity to allow you to operate at peak performances without wasting energy while achieving protection from the sun and making maximal use of your sweat for cooling.*

clothing layers and activities to allow you to operate at peak performances without wasting water and energy to sweating or shivering.

In hot climates, clothing protects you against direct radiation from the sun, hot winds, scorching ground temperatures, and a plethora of things that poke, bite, sting, or prick. Loose layers of the appropriate material grant protection from the sun and increase airflow while slowing the evaporation of sweat for superior cooling. The ideal scenario in the heat is to regulate layers and physical activity to allow you to operate at peak performances without wasting energy while achieving protection from the sun and making maximal use of your sweat for cooling.

Properties of Clothing Materials

Clothing is a detailed subject to which an entire book could be dedicated. What type of material your clothing is made from is extremely important. In today's world, there seems to be billions of trendy, new outdoor fabrics on the market, so much so that people fifty years ago must have stayed indoors, terrified of their inadequate clothing. Experiencing all the latest technical fabrics would require a second mortgage on the house and hours of free time. If you're a gear junkie, have fun and let me know what you think regarding their performance or lack thereof. If you're a hardcore mountaineer, unless you're an acclimated Nepalese, you'll more than likely need special stuff. For this book, however, and for the majority of outdoor folks, I'll stick to outlining the pros and cons of basic outdoor fabrics that have withstood the test of time. Keep in mind that the properties described are just as applicable for blankets and sleeping bags.

Cotton

Cotton is *hydrophilic*, meaning it transfers sweat from your skin to the material itself, thus it sucks at "wicking" wetness away from the skin. In fact, cotton loves moisture and will become damp simply when exposed to humid air. Once wet, it feels cold, loses 90 percent of its insulating properties, is a real bummer to dry out and wicks heat from you 25 times faster than when it's dry. In summary, wearing cotton clothing in the winter is a death wish. Yet, in scorching summer deserts, it's my fabric of choice for precisely the same reasons. Add to this cotton's decent abrasion resistance and its ability to block a reasonable amount of UV radiation, and you have some decent desert duds.

Polypropylene

Polypropylene resists absorbing moisture as it's *hydrophobic*, meaning it transfers moisture from the skin across the fabric itself to other clothes or the air so it actually dries from the inside out. This quality makes it awesome at wicking sweat away from the skin, thus it's popular as a base layer. Polypropylene feels soft and is relatively cheap and easy to care for. On the down side, wearing it a few days in a row while exercising will cause you to smell like a troll's crotch. Being synthetic, it also easily melts to skin while you are singing Christmas carols around the fire. Regardless of stench and pain, polypropylene's most insidious disadvantage, ironically enough, comes from its superior wicking abilities. In a nutshell, the stuff removes moisture away from skin so well that the wicking action uses more body energy from the survivor than other fabrics. Because of this, polypropylene should only be worn when energy loss is not critical.

Wool

Since it is essentially animal hair with empty cells that trap air, wool is a poor conductor. Its natural crimp and elasticity coupled with the fact that wool fibers are hollow make it a great insulator. It's hygroscopic, and readily absorbs moisture but suspends the water vapor within the fiber itself. While any moisture in wool or other fabrics decreases the insulation value, wool can suck up 35 to 55 percent of its weight in water before feeling cold and wet. Although it's a drag to dry out, wool actually retains more heat than synthetic fabrics as it dries. This fact, combined with a slower wicking rate, causes wool to use less body energy than polypropylene.

Various breeds of sheep produce various types of wool as not all wool is garment quality. A wool fiber under magnification looks like a heavily barbed, demonic spear tip. Aside from allergies, the barbs from the lesser breeds, along with potential sloppy manufacturing, cause the all-too-familiar "get this damn sweater off of me" itch. These same barbs allow wool fibers to be crafted into felt. Wool is inherently flame retardant: it won't melt to your skin when you're sleeping next to a fire and is more forgiving than synthetics when using fire to dry out damp clothing.

Sock it to me!

Cold feet, at one time or another, have been the bane of all outdoor recreationists. At a minimum, cold tootsies make an otherwise pleasant outing a drag. On the other side of the coin, you could lose toes or even your entire foot to frostbite. While I'll never write a book about footwear, I do have a fair amount of experience with socks. I have worn two to three pairs of "new" (holey socks don't cut it) wool socks, sans shoes or boots, for years in cold, dry snowy conditions with great results. Put on the smallest pair of socks first, and then one or two larger pairs over the first pair. I reserve the outer sock for the pair that has the most wear. While this might seem like insane behavior, learning more about why feet get cold is all the explanation you should need.

Why feet get cold:

1. The feet are located farthest from the heart, away from a warm, circulating blood supply.
2. Feet sweat a lot, up to a half a cup per day, thereby soaking a sock's insulation.
3. Most shoes and boots act as a vapor barrier that prevents sweat-soaked socks from drying.
4. Poorly fitting footwear, lacing boots too tightly, or trying to stuff a foot with two pairs of socks into a summer shoe or boot makes for a tight fit and impedes circulation. Foot circulation will already be compromised due to peripheral constriction of the blood vessels from outside cold temperatures.
5. The insulation the sock provides is compressed by footwear, and the fact that it's being stood upon.
6. Feet lose heat by conduction to cooler ground temperatures, and sweaty socks increase the conductive heat loss.

Donning loose and layered new wool socks allows for excess foot perspiration to freely evaporate while minimally compressing insulation and impeding circulation. Wool socks work best in cold, dry conditions (dry snow actually sucks the moisture from a water-logged sock) but I've worn them in slush as well. Experiment in your backyard to see what works for you. In the wilderness, if your ability to walk is compromised due to lost or damaged footwear, you might be headed for disaster. Two extra pairs of wool socks in your pack, kept dry in a freezer bag, might allow you to comfortably walk away from a deadly scene.

As if that's not enough, wool is able to neutralize many types of acids and chemical bases, which helps prevent the buildup of germs. On the down side, wool is bulky when compared to synthetics and requires more space in the pack.

Polyester

Polyester is by far the most widely used material in outdoor clothing, surpassing even my beloved wool. Polyester pile fabrics are good insulators, can absorb a fair amount of water without feeling cold, and are hydrophobic. The fibers themselves can be woven into many different thicknesses providing both insulation and wind-stopping abilities. They are more compact than wool and come in a wide variety of obnoxious colors perfect for being found. A true hippy success story, nearly 80 percent of polyester outdoor clothing is made from recycled plastic bottles.

A tried and true acronym for winter wear!

C = *keep yourself and clothes* CLEAN

O = *avoid* OVERHEATING

L = *wear clothes* LOOSE *and in* LAYERS

D = *keep* DRY

Nylon

Nylon is pretty tough stuff and is commonly used in the design of environmental layers. Spun tightly enough, it works well at repelling wind and water and can be made waterproof through various coatings available at outdoor stores, albeit at the expense of breathability. Nylon is extremely compact and lightweight and the little water it does absorb evaporates quickly.

Your environmental layer is critical, as a wind of merely nine miles per hour can reduce the effectiveness of clothing insulation by 30 percent. In addition to the wind chill, mixing wet clothing with the "bellows" effect produced by walking can compromise your clothing's insulation an unbelievable 85 percent!

Down

Down's compressibility, loft, and weight to warmth ratio are legendary. It is an amazing insulator when it's dry. Unfortunately, down is hydrophilic and sucks even more than cotton in cold, wet environments, losing virtually all of its insulative properties, and is nearly impossible to dry in the backcountry.

The art of putting on and taking off layers of clothing to regulate body temperature is amazingly simple, requiring very little practice and few calories and water from the survivor. In short-term survival, clothing's divine simplicity eliminates the necessity to create a fire. Fire is a task that requires fine and complex motor skills, physical dexterity, prior training, precious time, calories, and water from the survivor, dry tinder and adequate fuel, an ignition source, a safe spot to build, and constant monitoring. In a pinch, it's possible to improvise insulation from the natural world, depending upon the environment. Leaves, pine needles, dry grass, plant fibers, moss, and other material may be available. Since clothing is your lifeline for thermoregulating core body temperature, resist the temptation to play mountain man or woman, and visit the great outdoors fully equipped with adequate clothing.

Acclimatization

Now I'd like to add a personal word on clothing, or the lack thereof. Most of the time I don't wear much clothing. There are reasons for this. First, I live in Arizona. While Arizona is a land of extreme temperature fluctuations, below-zero temperatures are not typical in my direct environment. I can and do, however, experience them an hour away along with the 12,000-foot-plus mountain that creates them. Winter temperatures average from the mid-20s to the low 30s with many mornings starting out in the teens. Stuff freezes, it's windy, I can see my breath, and it snows. Local summer temperatures can climb in excess of 100°F (38°C). Drive an hour south into the desert and you can experience temperatures in excess of 120°F (49°C).

I lived in a yurt (a Mongolian tent) in my friend's backyard for several years. In the winter at night, my two-gallon water container would nearly freeze solid, requiring me to sleep with perishable food products such as fruits and vegetables in order to prevent them from becoming mush the next day. Another time in my life, while living in a brush shelter in the woods, I'd sit cross-legged in front of my thatched door, eating noodles while snow blew in the sides. To this day, after scraping winter ice from the windshield, I drive my Jeep early in the morning without using the heater.

In the summer, this same black Jeep has no air conditioning. In my yurt, I couldn't leave candles sitting in candleholders, as the intense heat would cause them to melt and fall over. Many days I would soak my cotton T-shirt with water to keep cool. I'd have to repeat the process every half-hour or so as the intense heat would quickly dry out my shirt. I didn't have chairs but would rather lie on the floor, taking advantage of the cooler air. I did and still do all this barefoot, in shorts and a T-shirt.

I relay this to illustrate that to a certain point, the human body can acclimate to temperature variation. Slow acclimatization through repeated exposure to hot and cold environments results in more active sweating in response to continued heat and an increase in subcutaneous fat deposits in response to cold. Chronic exercise in hot or cold environments also helps with the acclimatization process. Exercising in the heat, done with common sense, improves thermoregulation during hot weather in general by causing one to sweat quicker as well as increasing the total amount of sweat produced. In addition, training seems to cause existing sweat glands to get bigger without increasing the total number. Other adaptations include an increase in total blood volume and maximal cardiac output causing the blood flow in muscles and skin, with its heat flux, to be better preserved during strenuous exercise in hot weather. Stories of Tibetan monks sitting in the snow next to an icy mountain stream drying out wet sheets placed over their naked bodies is more common than not. Research involving Australian aborigines has shown that both skin and core temperatures drop (core temps lower to 95°F (35°C)!) when they sleep in the cold desert. Doing so reduces the temperature gradient between their skin and the colder environment, thereby reducing heat loss while conserving energy. I've seen several magazine photos of smiling little kids in some faraway country, standing barefoot in the snow and surrounded by a paper-thin blanket. At many of the primitive living skills conferences around the nation, naked babies run through grass thick with morning frost, oblivious to the cold, their buckskin-clothed parents trailing behind. A few generations past, people spent 90 percent of their life outdoors and 10 percent indoors. Today, the exact opposite is true.

Most of us "modern" folks have robbed ourselves of the experience of acclimatization for whatever reason. Instead, we put on extra clothing early in the season and take it off late when the season's passed. We saunter from climate-controlled shelters to climate-controlled vehicles to climate-controlled work areas to climate-controlled shopping centers, worshiping the almighty god called "room temperature." The body never has a chance to acclimate to temperature variation because it never needs to. But to each his or her own. There's nothing wrong with living a cli-

mate-controlled life; I'm simply explaining how and why I do what I do. I choose to acclimate as much as possible to the heat and cold for several reasons. I use myself as a human guinea pig to push the envelope of my own personal limits. There is a big difference between being uncomfortable and being dangerous when it comes to training in temperature extremes. Acclimatization is like weight training; you either use it or lose it. Unfortunately, the "losing it" part can happen fast.

I bathe less frequently when the weather turns cold, as there's less sweat and smell due to cooler air temperatures. By doing so, I notice a small difference in heat retention due to the increased buildup of natural protective oils secreted by the skin. This "micro coating" of oil, from my experience, makes the skin less susceptible to chilly convective breezes. (Don't confuse limited showering with "stink." I can still spot wash the crotch and underarms without prematurely removing this protective layer from the rest of my body.) As an added bonus, my skin doesn't become dry and flake as much when subjected to the cold, dry air of winter.

I also routinely wear the same T-shirt for three to five days in a row depending on my activity level. Obviously, the shirt's limited insulating properties soon plug up with body oil, dirt, or whatever else I've been doing. When I do finally change, I immediately notice the renewed insulating qualities of the fiber. The "clean" T-shirt, for me, feels like donning a light jacket. In addition, I tend to save new shirts for the winter as they're thicker and provide better insulation. Laugh if you will, but it works for me.

Short- and Long-Term Heat Production Methods

In its defense against the cold, the body has both short-term and long-term heat production methods. Examples of producing heat in the *short-term* include eating more food, especially simple sugars and some carbohydrates, muscular activity through shivering or exercise, and nonshivering thermogenesis.

Foods composed mostly of simple sugars as well as certain carbohydrates jump-start the body's metabolism by burning very quickly. Examples of this include candy and breads. Longer-lasting energy is squeezed from complex carbohydrates, such as beans, pasta, and oats, while even more sustained calories are extrapolated from proteins and especially fats. Fats have long been the food of choice for survival because of their high energy density, but consider adding more carbohydrates to maintain blood glucose levels because carbohydrates are digested and absorbed much more rapidly than fats. Eating smaller, more frequent meals increases the body's metabolism, thereby burning more calories for digestion, a process referred to as "diet-induced thermogenesis." This "Thermal Effect of Food" or "TEF" principle, in a nutshell, creates a higher metabolism, which in turn increases the amount of calories burned. These increased calories produce MORE HEAT for the survivor.

Human beings produce tremendous amounts of energy while exercising. As the physical activity increases, energy production climbs. Roughly 82 to 90 percent of the energy produced by exercising manifests itself as heat. In fact, muscle produces 100 times more heat at work than when at rest! Only a small portion of the heat produced through exercising is lost from the skin as most of the heat is passed to the body's core via flow of venous blood returning to the heart.

Exercising like a crazy person, however, quickly burns up your body's available glucose supply, forcing it to tear into and consume readily available glycogen reserves. Glucose, found in certain foods and in the normal blood of all animals, is the product of carbohydrate metabolism and is the "magic juice" of life, being the primary source of energy for living organisms. Extra glucose is converted to glycogen and stored in the muscles (350 to 475 grams) and liver (100 grams) for energy when needed and, beyond that, is converted to and stored as fat. Each gram of glycogen contains around four kilocalories of energy and is hydrated with 2.7 grams of water. When glycogen is used for energy by catabolism, this water is freed up to be used by the body. Water produced in this way is referred to as *metabolic water* and provides roughly 26 to 32 percent of the daily water requirement in a normal, sedentary person. The act of using up all available glucose and glycogen stores is sometimes referred to as "hitting the wall" and leaves you totally exhausted. With the body's carbohydrate stores vaporized and the threat of hypoglycemia (low blood sugar) looming just over the next hill, glucagon levels rise, insulin falls, and the body attempts to maintain blood glucose levels by synthesizing noncarbohydrates in the liver, a process referred to as *gluconeogenesis*. To prevent this, do what aerobics instructors have known for years—exercise at 60 percent of your maximal oxygen uptake or *VO2 max*. Doing so will cause your body to dig into its significantly larger fat storage deposits instead of using limited glycogen (carbohydrate) and glucose reserves. This means you can go farther and longer before becoming tired.

Consuming alcohol, especially in cold environments, is a no-no, as it impairs the ability of the liver to maintain blood-sugar levels, causing them to drop due to the glucose needed to metabolize the alcohol. This puts one at a greater risk for developing hypothermia. Alcohol, famous for allowing one to score high on the stupid meter, also decreases the shivering response, and causes one to feel less discomfort from hot and cold weather while completely trashing good judgment.

It doesn't take a genius to figure out that repetitive movements of the larger muscle groups, such as those in the butt and legs, can really make a difference in regulating body temperature. Exercising in the cold to the point of sweating is rife with problems, as we have discussed. The Inuit peoples of the Canadian Arctic have an old saying, "If you sweat, you die." Works for me.

During nonshivering thermogenesis, hormones are released that increase the metabolic activity in all the body's tissues. Heat is produced via a low-efficiency metabolic pathway in mitochondria that increases the production of heat by uncoupling the production of ATP from energy consumption. Mitochondria are your body's "furnaces" and are responsible for heat production. They are small organelles within the cell that are active in the transfer of energy during metabolism. They help turn fats, proteins, and carbohydrates into energy or ATP (Adenosine Triphosphate) and heat. Heat production is limited by the amount of carbohydrates available to the cells' mitochondria and the amount of oxygen that's allowed to reach the body's working muscles.

Long-term heat production involves three factors, one of which is increased appetite. Pigging out on more food leads to a higher metabolic rate, thus enhanced heat production. The liver, processing nutrients, is responsible for the majority of the increase, with the greatest bang for the buck coming from the assimilation of proteins. Metabolism is measured in watts. On an average, a person's basal metabolic rate (BMR), the amount of calories burned daily at rest, produces 100 watts. As mentioned previously, exercise produces tremendous heat, and can increase your 100-watt "light bulb" BMR to an astonishing 1,500 watts, a heating capacity on par with an electric space heater!

Most everyone has experienced the winter joys of eating till you nearly vomit. Thank God that Thanksgiving and Christmas are not in July. When I lived in the woods during the winter, I craved calories like a madman, especially nice gooey fats. Upon returning home in the evenings to my wickiup shelter, I'd grab a jar of peanut butter and gobble down two huge spoonfuls of the precious goo. My body craved extra energy as I was burning massive amounts of calories trying to keep warm with minimal clothing as well as using my bike and hiking as my primary means of transportation. Due mainly to a traditional diet rich in fats and proteins, Eskimos have a BMR that is up to 33 percent higher than European cultures!

The other two factors of long-term heat production are far more complex and interesting and revolve around acclimating to the cold. One involves raising the amount of mitochondria within the cells themselves. In essence, repeated exposure to cold increases the amount of mitochondria within your cells! It also increases the amount of fat your body burns while conserving carbohydrates, thus enabling you to expend greater amounts of energy before chewing up glucose and glycogen stores. This phenomenon, when coupled with a strict observance of the "60-percent rule" stated earlier, allows for very efficient, heat-

producing endurance. The more mitochondria you have, the more heat can be produced. Last but not least, repeated exposure to cold increases the action of nonshivering thermogenesis. Both offer no-bullshit scientific proof to the benefits of acclimatization.

A person's internal "temperature stability" depends on the ratio between his or her capacity for *heat production,* determined by volume, and his or her potential for *heat loss,* determined by surface area. I have a larger volume than many people and can limit my surface area by keeping arms at my sides, huddling, or whatever physical pose is necessary at the time.

The phrase "mind over matter" is a common one. Less common is an understanding about what it means. From my experience, there is something to be said about visualization and affirming what you'd like rather than what you're experiencing. This is a heavy subject and I don't want to get too groovy in this book. In any event, blending the physiology and physics behind body temperature regulation with the spiritual wisdom of several thousands of years can pack a potent punch.

If you wish to experiment with temperature acclimatization, please do it in the safety of your own backyard and don't be stupid about it. This type of training, at least for me, is merely meant to supplement being prepared in the first place. I am able to wear less clothing than most people I know in temperature extremes but always have along extra clothing should conditions require it. I know what works for me because I've been consciously practicing with my body for more than fifteen years. Know what works for you and stick to the plan, as I'd hate to walk over your dead body in the spring. **Remember: Clothing is your lifeline as it regulates core body temperature. It is your personal shelter and your first line of defense.** Forget this and you'll pay the ultimate price.

Water

Water is a biological necessity down to the cellular level. It is not an optional item. It's general knowledge that water accounts for nearly two-thirds of the body's total weight. It seems that the older we get, however, the drier we become. Floating around in the womb, overall body-water content was more than 80 percent. As a baby, the rate dropped to around 73 percent. In young adults, the body contains roughly 65 percent water, 70 percent in the muscles and 50 percent in fat deposits. Between 40 and 60 years old, water content drops to 55 percent for males and 47 percent for females. After 60, the rate drops even further, 50 percent for males and 45 percent for females.

Water has several amazing properties, including the fact that it's an excellent solvent. Water dissolves a remarkable number of inorganic molecules. When dissolved, the molecules break apart to form a solution. Living activities on a cellular level take place either dissolved in fats or water. Water has a high heat capacity, meaning it requires a lot of energy to heat it up or cool it down so it can handle a wide variety of outside temperature fluctuations within the cell before problems arise. The water in your blood helps the circulatory system get rid of excess heat or distribute heat to wherever it's needed during the cold. Digestion and metabolism are water-based processes, and water lubricates the joints and helps eliminate waste products from the body as well. Water is even required for the simple act of breathing, as the lungs need moisture to oxygenate blood and rid the blood of excess carbon dioxide. Nearly 70 percent of the earth's surface is covered in water. It is therefore no exaggeration to say that water is life itself.

My beloved desert can be so hot and dry that people don't seem to perspire. Since they're "not sweating," they underestimate how hot

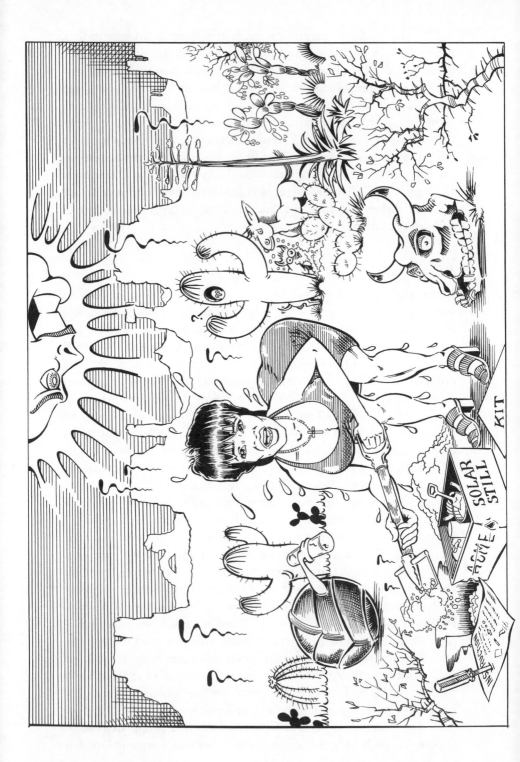

98.6 Degrees: The Art of Keeping Your Ass Alive!

the temperature really is and they ignore the urge to drink. The sinister truth is revealed by putting a hand on the skin for a minute or two. Lift the hand and it's sodden with sweat, proof enough at the body's desperate attempt to keep the brain and internal organs cool. In extremely hot temperatures, unprotected skin instantly loses moisture.

A person at rest loses a little more than a quart and a half of water every day. If you screw up and do everything wrong in a desert-survival situation, however, like attempting to free your car from a sand wash at noon, it's possible to lose a gallon of water an hour in sweat. A gallon of water weighs 8.3 pounds, depending on air temperature! Someone should tell Oprah. This heinous fact should make it readily apparent that the "standard survival recommendation" of carrying one gallon of water per person per day is completely bogus. I recommend at least three gallons per person per day, more if the terrain, temperatures, or activities undertaken are extreme. Seeing as how the average lifestyle consumes 116 gallons to 220 gallons of water every day, with some wealthy communities in my arid state using in excess of 400 gallons daily, it isn't hard to see our gross neglect regarding the importance of conserving the wet stuff. For every quart of sweat you lose, your heart rate raises about eight beats per minute, your cardiovascular system becomes more stressed, and your cooling system declines. In other words, dehydration sucks and greatly impedes your physical and psychological performance.

Exercising in the heat without fluid intake does not bestow upon you magical desert-adaptation qualities. In fact, progressive dehydration during exercise in hot climates reduces the sensitivity of the sweat rate/core temperature relationship, thus increasing your risk for heat illness and hyperthermia. It also causes you to become tired much more easily. The quicker you poop out, the less training you're able to accomplish so your quest for physiological adaptation goes down the toilet. In a nutshell, when you're dehydrated and you exercise at any given intensity, your body temperature rises faster.

Regardless of physical activity or whether you spend a lot of time outdoors, if you're alive, you're losing water. This "insensible perspiration," necessary for the health and suppleness of our skin, uses about 600 to 900 milliliters of water per day.

Deadly Dehydration

Seventy-five percent of humans are chronically dehydrated. Thirty-seven percent mistake the thirst mechanism for hunger pangs. Lack of hydration is the number one trigger of daytime fatigue. The list goes on and on. If you live in an arid region or one with oppressively high humidity, you know how tough it is to remain hydrated. Doing so takes a lot of work! Although at times it's hard to remember to drink, and then to drink enough, it is critical that you stay maximally hydrated.

Dehydration is deadly in hot and cold weather. When the blood in your circulatory system loses water, it gets thicker. Thick blood circulates slower and is harder for the heart to pump, and, in regard to temperature regulation, hinders the body's ability to lose excess heat or circulate needed heat. When the volume of blood and extracellular fluids decreases, water is literally sucked from the cells, causing them to shrink, thereby damaging cell membranes and the proteins inside. Platelets actually stick together in the blood due to a lack of plasma. The result is an increase in the naturally occurring salts in the remaining body fluids. Normal body fluid has a salt concentration of 0.9 percent. In contrast, urine contains 2 percent salt, plus toxic urea, while sea water has a whopping 3.9 percent. Many researchers feel that rising salt concentrations within the body are responsible for the punishing side effects of dehydration.

Although dehydration triggers the secretion of several water-conserving hormones, one of which reduces the amount of water lost in the urine, exposure to cold weather without protection increases urine production. When surface blood vessels constrict from the cold, reducing the circulatory system and increasing blood pressure, pressure sensors in the body perceive an increase in volume and stimulate urine production. To add insult to injury, when outside temperatures plummet, so does your kidneys' ability to concentrate urine. The end result is you lose more water.

Body functions are severely limited if you lose 10 percent of your weight due to dehydration yet physical, mental, and emotional impairments manifest with the slightest loss of water, especially in the heat. Losing just 2 percent of body weight in water compromises your overall judgement by 25 percent. Being outside in temperatures of 100°F (38°C) or more will cause you to lose another 25 percent! To summarize this horrible truth, the average hiker recreating in hot temperatures who is a quart and a half low on water is operating at half the person he or she usually is! In arid regions around the world, this is a very common occurrence. The water in your body affects your circulation, metabolism, good judgment, and overall attitude. Does this stuff sound familiar? If not, flip back a few pages and reread how fear inhibits your circulation, metabolic process, good judgment, and overall attitude. Holy double negative, Batman! Like a spiderweb, the first strand's connected to the last. Fiddle with one strand and the whole thing moves. Outdoor enthusiasts take heed. It would be hard to find a real-life survival scenario that did not involve the enemies of fear and dehydration.

Exotic Methods

What about solar stills, honking-huge, liquid-filled cacti, and other "exotic" methods of procuring water? At my school I teach them all. I teach them to drive home the point that if you fail to carry water with you or know with infinite certainty where to find it above ground, you risk death. Putting a bagel in a plastic bag on the dash of your car in the

How your body loses water

FACTORS INSIDE THE BODY	EFFECT	FACTORS OUTSIDE THE BODY
Physical Exertion Illness (fever)	Increased sweating	Hot temperatures High humidity
Physical Exertion Illness (fever)	Increased respiratory loss	Low humidity High wind speed Cold temperatures
Diuretics: alcohol/coffee/tea	Increased urine loss	Hypothermia
Diarrhea	Increased bowel loss	Hot temperatures Low humidity
	Increased insensible perspiration	High wind speed Low humidity
Bleeding	Increased blood loss	

summer is all the proof you'll need that the physics behind solar stills does in fact work. The danger comes when you foolishly take the high-school lab experiment into the field under stress, fatigue, and dehydration, coupled with uncountable outdoor variables and expect it to work . . . at all. Unfortunately, countless books on survival shamelessly tout solar stills as the next best thing since sliced bread. Many authors, judging from their plagiarized text from the old Air Force survival manual and bogus illustrations have never even bothered to build a still. Some photographs exhibit stills that are so poorly constructed that it's obvious they were quickly dug for nothing more than a convenient photo opportunity. Do I sound critical and harsh? I think not. Harsh to me is you and your family perishing of dehydration and hyperthermia because you trusted some idiot and bought their bullshit. When my students build solar stills, I keep track of the water they consume while doing so. Without exception, regardless of variables in terrain, weather, earth-water content, solar intensity, added plant material, still sizes, sealing, plastic angle, transparency, number of people, ambient air temperature, digging tools, and time, they *always* lose much more water in the form of sweat than the still provides.

So, how do you know if you have enough water in your system? **Thirst should never be an indicator of when or how much to drink.** Being thirsty is a sign that you're already a quart to a quart and a half low. To make matters worse, somewhere down the line in Dehydrationville, the thirst mechanism stops working altogether.

There is no adaptation to dehydration. Military personnel have learned the hard way that "being tough" is not an acceptable substitute for water. Even the most seasoned special warfare soldier can and does fall prey to the punishment of dehydration. Through decades of accumulated training knowledge, the military unearthed the rare gem of "voluntary dehydration." It was repeatedly observed during outdoor training exercises in hot weather that soldiers would not drink enough water to take care of their needs, even when unlimited fluids were readily available! For some reason, they simply had no motivation to drink. This of course led to a downward spiral in efficiency as the soldiers stumbled deeper and deeper into dehydration. In order to avoid this process, soldiers were forced to drink more water than they wanted. It wasn't until training ceased and they were back in the relative comfort of their barracks chewing on a pizza that they drank the fluid their bodies so desperately craved. The moral of this story should be as clear as your urine: If you fart around outside in hot temperatures, drink more water than your body seems to want, much more water! If you're with company, watch them like a hawk and make sure they drink adequate fluids. It only takes one person to compromise the whole group.

As hinted at above, *the best way to tell if you're maximally hydrated is the color of your urine.* It should be as clear as a Rocky Mountain stream with no color whatsoever. Certain medications and vitamins color urine. Vitamins, especially B vitamins, color urine to the point where you could rent yourself out to a nightclub as a neon sign. The frequency and volume of urine produced by someone who has been drinking copiously are other hydration indicators although not as reliable as color. Using the three together will provide the most effective guesstimating as to when and how much you should drink. All proteins require water for digestion, so back off on consuming the lobster tails and elk burgers if the wet stuff is scarce.

Four Factors for Faster Hydration: Hydrating quickly for maximal efficiency at work or in the woods

There are four factors to consider for achieving maximal hydration in the shortest amount of time. While it's nearly impossible to obtain all four in the field, it's quite easy in the office. Corporate efficiency consultants take heart!

Four Factors for accelerated maximal hydration

1. Adequate volume.
2. Temperature.
3. Minimal salts, carbohydrates, and sugars.
4. Carbonation.

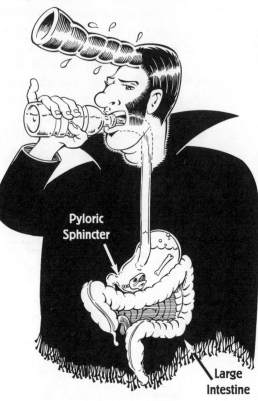

Pyloric Sphincter

Large Intestine

Adequate Volume

Take a swig of water and this sacred substance runs down your esophagus and into your stomach. Water sitting in your stomach doesn't mean squat as the stomach does nothing to absorb this wonderful fluid into your body. The trick to maximal hydration in the shortest amount of time is to blow water past your stomach and small intestine and into the large intestine where it's absorbed. Drinking an adequate volume of water (in other words, feeling like a bloated pig) coerces the stomach into shooting it past the opening between your stomach and small intestine, called the *pyloric sphincter*. Most people are routinely a quart or more low on water. At the start of my field courses, I have students drink at least a quart or two before venturing into the bush. I have them drink to the point of feeling slightly nauseous. Going beyond this is counterproductive, and we have to start all over again. I minimize their psychological discomfort by reminding them that a camel has the ability to chug up to 120 quarts of water in less than 10 minutes. Although they whine and moan at first, after fifteen minutes of hiking they feel like a million bucks.

Temperature

Your body is a very temperature-sensitive creature and likes things done its way. Due to this sensitivity, it stands to reason that dropping temperature extremes into its depths will affect your overall performance. To prove the point, look no further than the glaring example of eating copious amounts of snow contributing to hypothermia. Water that is tepid, or near body temperature, to cool is the most rapidly absorbed by your body. However, in cold weather, warming water to as hot as you can drink helps keep your core temperature stable. Conversely, folks in a hot-weather scenario would benefit from drinking very cool water. Quickly drinking large amounts of cold water can give rise to stomach cramping and, in more serious cases of dehydration, cause you to barf up the goods, so use caution.

If all this sounds like a lot of common sense, you win the new car. Water temperature is a factor in rapid absorption but should not stop you from drinking hot water in hot weather or cold water in cold weather. Rarely will you encounter cool water in the desert or warm water in the high mountains in January. I'm simply presenting your best possible options. You would have to be well prepared to reap all the benefits of quick, maximal water-absorption techniques but, after all, proper preparation is what this book is all about.

Minimal Salts, Carbohydrates, and Sugars

Drinking fluids containing minimal salts, carbohydrates, and sugars helps prevent your body from treating your water like food. The stomach and small intestine absorb nutrients from whatever you put in your mouth—that's their job. As we have already discussed, for the fluid you drink to be absorbed and stave off dehydration, it must reach the large intestine. The more food-stuff water possesses, the longer it hangs out in the stomach and small intestine digesting.

A barrage of sports drinks exist on the market, many backed by big-money advertising campaigns. All contain a fierce amount of salt, carbohydrates, and sugar. Electrolyte replacement can be an issue in long-term survival but pales in comparison to dying of short-term dehydration. Add human nature to the mix and powdered electrolyte replacements can ruin your day. My hometown fire department stopped using dry electrolyte replacements because of the false belief that more is better. Regardless of the fact that the directions said to use one scoop per gallon, they used 2, 3, or even 4 scoops per gallon. Because they lacked the water in their systems to process the excessive electrolytes being ingested, they overdosed and got sick. Sports medicine colleges around the nation have completed study after study on hydration and most recommended plain old water. One concluded that the most-efficient mix for marathon runners was a gallon of water mixed with two tablespoons of apple juice. Of the many electrolyte-replacement solutions tested, most were successful at increasing hydration simply because they tasted better than straight water, thus the subject tended to drink more, and more often. Whatever works. To add to the confusion, current research says that although stomach emptying is delayed by sugar, the absorption rate in the large intestine is slightly increased by lightly sweetened drinks. For me, sugary liquids in the outdoors on a regular basis aren't worth the hassle because water bottles become sticky, a drag to clean, and attract every bee and yellow jacket this side of the Continental Divide.

Regardless, the most important factor is drinking a lot of water, even if it's laced with trace nutrients. On desert-survival courses, I sometimes add flavoring to the funky water we find, which is usually warm or hot, and can sport anything from cow dung to decomposing animals. Flavoring the strange brew helps me to get it down and keep it down, and allows me to drink massive quantities of otherwise truly nasty water. My favorite flavorings are the cherry and grape Kool-Aid packets with added sugar. Stay away from all alcoholic products—alcohol increases dehydration by eliminating more fluid from the body through the kidneys than the quantity of liquid you originally consumed. After all, alcohol is a toxin and requires eight ounces of plain water to neutralize one ounce of it. If electrolyte solutions trip your trigger, so be it, but consider diluting the overall concentration with added water.

Carbonation

While undoubtedly the toughest to obtain in the field, the pressure built up from drinking carbonated liquid helps shoot it past the stomach's pyloric sphincter and into the open arms of your water-absorbing large intestine. Packing along some Alka-Seltzer tablets is a quick and dirty way to carbonate water with just a hint of sodium, which is a potential asset in hot weather as long as you have plenty of water. Pack the stuff without added aspirin and look for the generic version to save cash. By the time you blast out your first belch, your pyloric sphincter will have already opened, so congratulations! Remember, these water-absorption tips are in NO WAY meant to stop you from drinking water that doesn't pass the test. (I'll be pissed if I hear you died of dehydration next to a full cattle tank because you didn't have a case of cool, carbonated bottled water with a pinch of apple juice!)

Hauntingly Hideous Hyponatremia

Regardless of my pro-water stance, at times, drinking too much water without an adequate salt intake can cause problems. Sodium (salt) is a required element for the body to function properly and is lost in sweat and urine. Hyponatremia means a low concentration of sodium in the blood and can pose a real threat to survivors who exert themselves in a hot environment. It's caused by lost sweat, (salt and water) being replaced by only water (no salt) thus diluting the sodium in the bloodstream, a phenomenon commonly experienced by ultra-endurance runners. Over time, salt lost from the body doesn't get replaced as quickly as lost water, and long-term exercise in the heat causes more salt to be lost from the body than would normally be replaced by food and sports drinks. The Grand Canyon National Park recently posted warning signs at trailheads alerting unacclimated "green-horn" visitors to the dangers of chugging too much water while hiking without adequate salty foods. Unfortunately, symptoms mimic dehydration and may include nausea, muscle cramps, disorientation, slurred speech, confusion, and in later stages, seizures, coma, and death. Use additional caution when taking aspirin, ibuprofen, acetaminophen (Tylenol) and other anti-inflammatory medications that mess with kidney functions, as these agents may further compound hyponatremia. The good news is that minor hyponatremia can be effectively treated (or the problem avoided altogether) by eating extra salty foods or adding a small amount of table salt to drinking water when necessary.

Precious Stuff

Of the 1,700 million square miles of water on planet Earth, all 326 million trillion gallons of it, less than 0.5 percent is potable. Ninety-eight percent of our planet's water is composed of ocean, 2 percent is fresh but locked up in the form of glaciers, and another 0.36 percent is found underground. In fact, only 0.036 percent of the earth's entire water supply is found in our lakes and rivers.

The United Nations estimates that there are currently 1.1 million people worldwide who live without access to safe drinking water. Regardless of these facts, we poop and pee in the wet stuff every chance we get. Field methods of water disinfection and filtration have become increasingly important, largely due to the current invasion of people entering our nation's backcountry. On an average, we produce half a pound of crap per person every day. Illness-causing pathogens in fecal matter can survive for months underground and travel more than 300 feet through the earth, contaminating above- and below-ground water sources with a host of nasties. Even well-seasoned outdoor folks, at one point or another, have dropped their drawers in an ecologically compromising locale. In canyon country, this is sometimes hard to avoid. Practicing sound sanitation skills in the wilderness, encouraging alternative sanitation options in our towns and cities, and speaking out against rampant development will help us protect what pure water sources we have left.

In summary, the only way your body loses heat when exposed to high temperatures is by sacrificing water in the form of sweat, which then evaporates upon the skin. In hot temperatures without water, dehydration and hyperthermia can rapidly cause your death.

It seems too simple that clothing and water can accomplish so much, but it's true. Have adequate clothing and water for the area you'll be traveling in, leave a game plan with two trusted people about where you're going and when you'll be back, know how to signal for rescue, and cultivate and maintain a "Party On" attitude. This is minimal. The icing on the cake is having a good survival kit and knowing how to use it. But even then there are no guarantees.

ABOUT YOUR RESCUERS: AN INTRODUCTION TO YOUR SAVING GRACE

*T*ypically, if you make it through a survival situation alive, it's because you were rescued by another party. This party is generally a Search and Rescue or SAR unit. SAR units come in a variety of shapes, colors, and sizes as programs, equipment, and personnel differ geographically in accordance with local needs and resources available. Where I live, in Yavapai County, Arizona, there exists a plethora of SAR groups, many with specialized training in a particular arena. Yavapai County is larger than the state of Rhode Island, comprising more than 8,300 square miles, (the seventh largest county in the United States) with geography ranging from high-altitude fir forest to lower Sonoran desert. It is one of the busiest for SAR missions in the state. To compensate for the massive terrain variables and the sheer number of callouts, many different units are needed, including dogs, scuba, 4 x 4, helicopter and airplane, ground trackers, swift water and cave rescue, mounted (horse back), and a backcountry unit that does about everything under the sun.

The National Search and Rescue Plan is a federal document that's the basis for the National Search and Rescue Manual, which contains information pertaining to organizations, methods and techniques, and various resources. Regardless of the feds, and assuming your last name is not Kennedy, local and state agencies are expected to mobilize the initial search response within their scope of ability, resources, and geography.

SAR organizations are the responsibility of national parks, state parks, county sheriffs, or state conservation officers, depending on the particular state or park. In Arizona, the task falls upon the shoulders of the sheriff of each county. Thus, those responsible for initially organiz-ing your rescue are paid sheriff's-office personnel. The vast majority of people searching for you, however, are volunteers. Having a paid, fully staffed SAR team on call 24/7 would bankrupt virtually any state in our union. Therefore, from coast to coast, the system relies heavily upon volunteers. In fact, volunteers conduct 99 percent of all ground-based search and rescue operations nationwide. Most of these people take their work very seriously, working long, hard hours with little or no recognition while being subject to the same risks and environmental hazards as the victim. Their rescue service motto is "These Things We Do That Others May Live," and they should be heartily commended for their selflessness as they offer a true service to humanity. The number of people searching for you will vary as not all volunteers can rearrange their lives at the drop of a hat and available resources may be stretched to the limit. The Grand Canyon racks up more than 400 SAR opera-tions each year alone! Although the exact number of SAR missions is impossible to figure, as no agency is responsible for gathering such data, estimates are in excess of 100,000 annually.

Search and Rescue is complex, dynamic, and always changing. What might be standard operation one year may be heavily modified the next. As more information is gathered and technology evolves, so does the way SAR conducts its business. Just about anything imagina-ble may be used on a SAR mission depending upon availability and the creativity of those in charge. Specialized personnel used in the past have included communications experts, chemists, rock climbers, inter-viewers, physicians, cavers, and even witches, prophets, and diviners! Special equipment could include attraction devices such as lights, sirens, horns, and flags as well as military mine detectors, Global Positioning Systems (GPS), Emergency Locator Transmitters (ELT), noise-sensitive equipment, night-vision goggles, and infrared devices such as "for-ward-looking infrared" (FLIR) on aircraft.

SAR involves two sets of disciplines, *search* and *rescue*. The search involves locating your missing butt and is made simpler and quicker if you leave a game plan with two responsible people. The easier you are to locate and rescue, injuries aside, the quicker you'll be savoring that cappuccino at home. *The more visible you and your party are to searchers, the greater your chance of being found.* I know of a woman who used her laptop computer screen at night to get the attention of rescuers. Brilliant! Work hard at becoming extremely visible, having the greatest amount of attraction. In other words, be as obnoxious as possible!

Rescue involves getting your body out of God knows what situation,

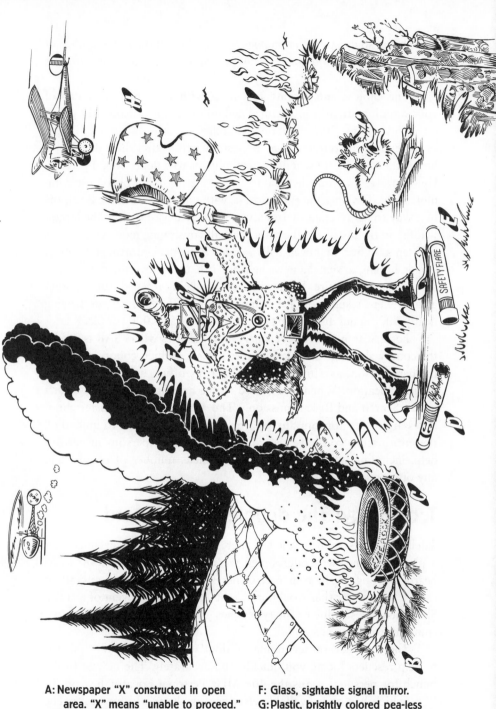

A: Newspaper "X" constructed in open
   area. "X" means "unable to proceed."
B: Green vegetation makes white smoke.
C: Petroleum products make black smoke.
D: Aerial signal flare.
E: Road flare.

F: Glass, sightable signal mirror.
G: Plastic, brightly colored pea-less
   whistle.
H: Hallmarks of successful signaling:
   CONTRAST and MOVEMENT.
I: "Groups of three" indicate distress.

some being so dynamic that movies are based upon them. Regardless of modern transportation methods, 90 percent of all rescues are carryouts on foot.

The choices and actions you make within the first six hours of your situation are the most critical and influence the outcome the greatest. In my county, 90 percent of all searches are solved within 12 hours, or less commonly referred to as a "hasty search." After three days or 72 hours, the "successful search" rate plummets to a depressing 3 percent. Use whatever's at your disposal to attract attention but please use common sense. Torching the entire forest, with you in the middle, is not the best way to get rescued. Arizona was recently devastated by the largest wildfire in the history of the state. This all-consuming monster began as two separate fires that eventually merged into one. Unfortunately, a lost person hoping to signal a news helicopter that was covering the first fire started the second fire. While successful in being rescued, this person's actions were responsible for helping torch 469,000 acres, destroying nearly 500 homes and forcing the evacuation of 30,000 people.

For a Search and Rescue emergency, in states where SAR is run by the county sheriff, call 911. If you're not sure which county the missing person is in, ask for the county sheriff's office, and give them the victim's location. When transferred to the appropriate sheriff, say, "I have a Search and Rescue mission." The dispatcher will transfer you if necessary to the appropriate department. Now's the time to unload all the information you have regarding the person or persons in need of help, including where, when, type of vehicle, number of people, and any other relevant details.

Technology: The double-edged sword

Satellite rescue systems in the U.S. were born in the early seventies after a plane carrying two congressmen went down in Alaska, never to be heard from again. In response, Congress required all U.S. aircraft to carry a transmitter that would broadcast a signal in the event of a crash. Since then, the satellite rescue system has grown to more than thirty-two countries worldwide.

There are several technological doodads on the market designed to help rescuers locate you quickly and accurately. The newest of the bunch for personal use is the 406 MHz Personal Locator Beacon, or PLB, which has been available elsewhere in the world for years. The PLB, proven effective time and time again, is a one-pound, pocket-sized emergency beacon based on a smaller version of the EPIRB (Emergency Position Indicating Radio Beacon) and ELT (Emergency

Locator Transmitter) that boaters and pilots have used for years. The PLB sends out two signals, one alerting satellites to your general location while the other emits a homing signal to guide rescuers to your precise whereabouts. Each beacon is registered using a one-of-a-kind digital code so rescuers know exactly who is lost and who to contact as far as family and friends. Lower-end models are expected to retail from $300 to $500.

There is no question that technical rescue gear has saved hundreds of lives. There is also no question that it has been, and always will be, abused. Since the advent of the personal cell phone, the stupidity of human nature has spawned an entirely new generation of gene-pool hang-ons that otherwise would have provided valuable fertilizer. SAR personnel have responded to countless false-alarm blasphemes, such as running out of water or cigarettes, to those who were "lonely" and needed to talk, stretching an already thin volunteer system even thinner. While valuable in their proper context, if you dare trust your life entirely to a battery-dependent, fragile, mechanical gizmo, you no longer need to continue reading this book. If the weather is poor, or its dark and the terrain is difficult, rescue teams may be forced to delay their search, regardless of how much you paid for your stuff at the outdoor store.

More often than not, technical crutches are directly responsible for a person's mishap in the first place as the false sense of security they provide causes one to venture farther and farther down the path of no return, literally. The phenomenon is similar to one who has acquired their first four-wheel-drive vehicle. Having little or no experience with their new toy and its limitations, they soon find themselves buried up to the frame in mud or snow. Virtually gone is personal responsibility with the glib assumption that no matter what asinine act is accomplished, someone will bail me out if I push this button or pull this cord. Also growing at an alarming rate among outdoor enthusiasts is the affliction "cell-phone-itis." With cell phone in hand, they blissfully enter the woods with nothing else, carrying no other gear whatsoever, putting 100 percent of their confidence into a fickle, battery-dependent machine. A recent report from the Federal Communications Center stated that up to 70 percent of 911 calls made from cell phones were made unintentionally through speed dialing, unlocked phone keypads, and automatic dialing features! The blunders waste thousands of hours of emergency operators' time, and further stretch limited public-safety resources.

Each and every rescue mission puts SAR personnel into the same poop soup as their client, exposing them to countless environmental hostilities. Unfortunately, the "dumb disease" affects more than the general public. I've had people in a position of power—people who should know better—compromise the training and lives of others by sacrificing preparedness upon the altar of the great god technology. The current technology of the day, no matter how colorful, will never replace common sense and proper preparedness through quality survival training, training that ultimately teaches how to avoid outdoor calamities in the first place.

Take this advice for what it's worth. While emergency rescue devices are a godsend, please use them with a great sense of responsibility, common sense, and reserve.

HELPING RESCUERS BRING YOU BACK ALIVE: LEAVING RESCUERS A 5-W GAME PLAN FROM DAY HIKES TO EPIC BACKCOUNTRY BONANZAS

his book is based upon the fact that someone will be tracking you down if you screw up. They are looking for you because you bothered leaving a game plan before you left. *Get in the habit of leaving an itinerary regarding your whereabouts with two people you trust, before each and every outing.* We've already addressed the deadly day-hike scenario, but ponder also the location of your excursion.

There's a popular hiking spot in my town that's so profoundly urban that at the base of the mountain butte itself sprouts entire neighborhoods. The route is so well-used the city paved it, literally, with blacktop, allowing couples to push baby strollers up the trail.

Years back, hikers found the remains of human bones in the area, bones that apparently belonged to a man visiting on a business trip. He had decided to take a simple day hike and visit our town's glorious landmark. Unfortunately, in his apparent zeal to fully enjoy a southwestern view, he moved a little too close to the mountain's edge and promptly fell off. He didn't bother leaving a note with the hotel front desk as he was only going to be gone for a few hours. A day or two later, his wife reported him missing, filled with the absolute terror that only a lost loved one can conjure forth. Although distressed by her husband's unknown whereabouts, the months and years went by, and little by little she started to heal. Eventually, people found her husband's decomposed remains and the magic of dental identification enabled her to grieve all over again.

A simple note left with the hotel lobby might have spared his life or at least eliminated years of unnecessary pain and suffering for his wife and family. Think about it. If it's time for you to meet your maker, that's one thing, but be courteous enough to give the people who love you a break by allowing them to mourn only once. Considering the fact that simple day hikes kill far more people every year than backcountry treks, it's rudely apparent that it doesn't take a trip to the farthest reaches of the wilderness for you to appear very dead.

Search and Rescue are two different disciplines. If you've left a game plan and stuck to it, the time needed to search should be minimal, as you've already informed rescuers as to your location. Once you're found, the rescue happens as it needs to happen.

If you don't tell someone where you are going and when you will be back, no one will know you're missing. As an added slap in the face, if folks eventually do figure out you're missing, they'll have no idea where to search for you. Using the list below, prepare a plan for *two trusted people* (not the guy at the bar), including as much detail as possible. Instruct these folks to contact whoever handles Search and Rescue upon your failure to arrive back on time. The more detailed information the plan provides, the more efficient the rescuers will be able to do their job. While by no means exhaustive, this list serves as a sound guideline for most everyone.

Tell the following to at least two people you trust:

WHERE you will be going

I can't emphasize this point enough. Leaving a photocopy of a 7.5-minute topographical map with your destination and route of entry highlighted with a marker is ideal. Topographical maps are hard to beat for accuracy, as they illustrate in great detail hills, valleys, rivers, springs, cattle tanks, and a plethora of other geographical information. Search and Rescue personnel will most likely be using the same maps. If this method is impractical, explain the country you'll be visiting by creating a homemade map. I usually draw and label a picture map that could stand on its own, plus write a written list explaining my destination in bullet type, one- or two-line statements. Assume nothing regarding your rescuers

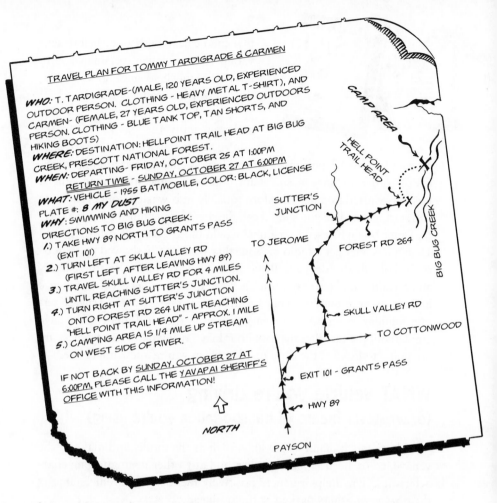

TRAVEL PLAN FOR TOMMY TARDIGRADE & CARMEN

WHO: T. TARDIGRADE-(MALE, 120 YEARS OLD, EXPERIENCED OUTDOOR PERSON. CLOTHING - HEAVY METAL T-SHIRT), AND CARMEN- (FEMALE, 27 YEARS OLD, EXPERIENCED OUTDOORS PERSON. CLOTHING - BLUE TANK TOP, TAN SHORTS, AND HIKING BOOTS)

WHERE: DESTINATION: HELLPOINT TRAIL HEAD AT BIG BUG CREEK, PRESCOTT NATIONAL FOREST.

WHEN: DEPARTING- FRIDAY, OCTOBER 25 AT 1:00PM
RETURN TIME - SUNDAY, OCTOBER 27 AT 6:00PM

WHAT: VEHICLE - 1955 BATMOBILE, COLOR: BLACK, LICENSE PLATE #: **8 MY DUST**

WHY: SWIMMING AND HIKING

DIRECTIONS TO BIG BUG CREEK:
1.) TAKE HWY 89 NORTH TO GRANTS PASS (EXIT 101)
2.) TURN LEFT AT SKULL VALLEY RD (FIRST LEFT AFTER LEAVING HWY 89)
3.) TRAVEL SKULL VALLEY RD FOR 4 MILES UNTIL REACHING SUTTER'S JUNCTION.
4.) TURN RIGHT AT SUTTER'S JUNCTION ONTO FOREST RD 264 UNTIL REACHING "HELL POINT TRAIL HEAD" - APPROX. 1 MILE
5.) CAMPING AREA IS 1/4 MILE UP STREAM ON WEST SIDE OF RIVER.

IF NOT BACK BY SUNDAY, OCTOBER 27 AT 6:00PM, PLEASE CALL THE YAVAPAI SHERIFF'S OFFICE WITH THIS INFORMATION!

⬆
NORTH

CAMP AREA

HELL POINT TRAIL HEAD

SUTTER'S JUNCTION

TO JEROME

FOREST RD 264

BIG BUG CREEK

SKULL VALLEY RD

TO COTTONWOOD

EXIT 101 - GRANTS PASS

HWY 89

PAYSON

being able to understand your drawing or read your writing. For multi-day treks, map as much of your journey as practical with a highlighter, including what day you'll reach each base camp and how long you'll be there. I know at times this is impossible, so don't make it more complex than necessary. Simply tell two people where you're going and make sure they understand their role should you fail to return as scheduled.

WHEN you will return

This little detail commences the initial response from rescuers. If someone knows where you are, but doesn't know your return time, you might be in for a long wait. I recommend you build in added time for the return trip. For example, if you plan to come back at noon, give yourself three to six hours to play with and say you'll return at 3 P.M. or 6 P.M. This allows extra time to have fun, fix the flat tire, or accomplish whatever might happen

that can be dealt with alone before activating tons of rescue personnel. Give rescuers as much advance notice as possible in which to conduct their search. If your buddy said he'd return at noon, and you notify the sheriff at 10 P.M., you've wasted away hours of daylight coveted by all SAR personnel. All wilderness emergencies are time-sensitive in order to have a successful outcome, some more than others. Precious wasted minutes transform quickly into wasted hours. The time you start feeling like you should call the sheriff *is* the time to call the sheriff. Don't be shy! Rescue personnel would much rather be called out and 15 minutes later get a radio message that your buddy showed up than be robbed of valuable daylight. Regardless of being overdue, weather factors and terrain variables may push back the time searchers will commence looking for your buddy. If your friend or loved one is traveling rugged terrain familiar to an SAR unit in which even the local guidebooks have erred about the fact that the "six-hour hike" really takes ten, rescuers are not going to leave at the drop of a hat when you're a few hours late.

WHAT vehicle you're driving
(or whatever means of transportation you're using)

Include as much detail as possible, such as the model and make of the vehicle, color, license plate number, and any other distinguishing characteristics. This helps rescuers positively identify your vehicle among the dozens of others parked at the trailhead.

WHO is in your party

Ground trail made by six people looks very different from one created by a lone hiker. Males and females have different backcountry habits and travel patterns, as do various age groups, so include this information as well as each person's general outdoor experience and clothing. In some cases, adding details regarding medical conditions or important medications is a wise move. Furthermore, to aid rescuers in "calling out" at the search site, include the full names of each person in your tribe.

WHY you're taking the trip

The activity you pursue in the backcountry, whether it's hiking, caving, canoeing, mountain biking, or mushroom picking will give rescuers an idea of what gear you might have and what factors might influence your behavior in regard to route finding, campsite location, and attraction to geographical features unique to an area.

The tin-foil tip-off

Unless you've achieved the power of levitation, some part of the body, most probably your feet, will be in contact with the ground while hiking. By taking a heavy-duty piece of tinfoil, placing it on soft ground, and firmly stepping on it with whatever boot or shoe you'll be wearing, you leave behind an effective imprint pattern for rescuers to follow. (If the ground is hard, use a towel or extra piece of clothing underneath the tinfoil.) At a glance they'll have the exact outline of your foot shape, size, and sole pattern, thus saving valuable time in trying to sort out your prints from the mishmash on the trail. If you're with a group of people, simply write your name above your impression and have everyone else do the same. Leave the imprints on your dashboard or some other easily viewed locale for rescuers to find. Do not leave a visible note displaying your return time or you'll find your hubcaps at the local swap meet.

Upon safe return, remember to notify your two trusted people so they don't contact rescue personnel! Leaving an accurate game plan before each and every outing is your ace in the hole for activating the Search and Rescue system. This fact alone could very well mean the difference of life or death for you or a loved one.

Introducing the typical SAR victim

The following passage was too juicy to pass up. Read it carefully and be honest with yourself, and remember, the very fact that you're reading this book proves you're on the right path to proper preparation.

"The average SAR victim is a composite outdoorsman (for example, hunter, fisherman, skier, hiker, climber, boater, photographer). Most do not do any of these activities well and are not members of organized groups that specialize in these pursuits. Most reside in densely populated areas and travel some distance for recreation and outdoor pursuits. They usually travel too fast and too far to acclimatize well to the terrain, altitude, and environmental conditions encountered. Interviews show that they also generally ignore signs of weather change, environmental hazards, body indicators, and written warnings concerning danger or safety."

Factors Contributing to Survival Situations and Search and Rescue Missions

- Improper clothing, footgear, or both.
- Lack of rest (fatigue).
- Lack of adequate water (dehydration).
- Hypothermia or hyperthermia.
- Too ambitious an undertaking for skills or proficiency.
- Poor physical condition, lack of motivation, or both.
- Inadequate or improper food.
- Little or no planning.
- Inadequate party for the goal, and lack of leadership.
- Itinerary confusing or not known to others.
- Individuals could not recognize a physical, mental, or environmental threat.
- No preparation for adverse weather.
- Unfamiliarity with terrain and lack of map or compass.
- "It can't happen to me" philosophy.

Gratefully reprinted with permission from
Wilderness Medicine, published by Mosby.

WHAT IS A SURVIVAL KIT?

survival kit is a distillation of the most-effective and simple means of staying alive. In it rests the tools that could make or break your life.

Kits can and should vary with the needs of the owner; thus, one carried by a Canadian bush pilot might look radically different from an earthquake kit in a southern California closet. However, the fact that we're in human bodies on a physical planet dictates that many components, while they may look different, provide the same functions.

Making Your Own Kit as Opposed to Purchasing One

The one-size-fits-all survival kit does not exist. There are plenty of kits on the market, and while I haven't seen them all, the majority of those that I have seen need help. While some components are non-negotiable, regardless of your situation, people are different and therefore have different needs. Many personal needs are subtle, but in a life-threatening circumstance, these subtleties count. In my opinion, you will fare much better if you put together your own. Creating a custom kit has the following advantages.

1. *You're guaranteed that the kit meets your personal needs.* The majority of the market sells products by hooking a person's ignorance, fear, and ego. The outdoor retail gear scene is a multimillion-dollar industry and the rules are no different. Compiling your own kit will allow you to buy or make top-quality items as needed; therefore, the knife you carry will be one you've chosen yourself, not one "Joe Blow" thought you should carry.

2. *You will be knowledgeable about what you're carrying.* Many commercial kits are "sealed for your protection" for whatever reason,

and allow you less of a chance to explore the contents. If you do buy a commercial survival kit, rip the little devil apart and see what you're proposing to lug around. Find out now if the thing the manufacturer calls a knife is really a razor blade, the snare wire is really two baggy ties, and the signal mirror is really a piece of tinfoil. Don't you dare buy a commercial kit and shove it under the car seat without inspecting the goods! Thoroughly check it out, as the last things needed in a compromising situation are more compromises.

3. *You are more apt to know how to use the components.* Although it's possible to design an outfit using components you don't know how to use, the likelihood of this happening in a homemade kit is much less than for a commercial one.

4. *You can replace worn-out or used items easier.* Devising your own setup allows you to practice using what you carry until you virtually wear out the stuff. With a homemade kit, buying new items is easy because you bought or made them yourself initially. Ready-made kits are often dependent upon bizarre gizmos manufacturers bought on sale back in the '90s at some outdoor show in Chicago.

5. *You'll gain the peace of mind and confidence of knowing that your kit is a part of you.* You know it has been prepared as well as possible and is ready for action if necessary. (It also saves legal fees if you bite the big one due to kit failure, as there's no one to sue!)

6. *You eliminate becoming the victim of a bad idea by yet another wanna-be, urban-armchair survival instructor with limited field experience.* All too frequently, survival equipment is designed and tested in air-conditioned offices or other temperate areas without any thought given to the oftentimes crappy conditions faced by the user. Extreme changes in temperature sometimes alter not only the user's dexterity, but the kit material itself. As an example, marine flares were wrapped in plastic that tore easily in a warm room but became stiff, tough, and slippery when exposed to cold water. One after-market test featured a Special Forces soldier who opened the flare package within seven seconds while in a warm and cozy environment. After spending an hour and fifteen minutes in 54°F water (12°C), the soldier required two minutes to open the package. To top it off, he couldn't manage the twisting motion to fire the flare because his hands were numb!

7. *Last but not least, anyone who stands to make a profit at your expense will be biased about his or her merchandise.* Face it—they have made a product they wish to sell in order to make money. To make a profit, many units must be quickly produced and then sold to a num-

ber of buyers. The maker will not be holding your hand if something goes wrong in the field.

There are decent kits out there and having one is certainly better than having none at all, but preparing your own kit or modifying a commercial one is a matter of taking responsibility for your own life. If you frequent the outdoors and can't find the time or ambition to put together a kit that could save your life or the life of someone you love, then maybe your gene pool should end with you.

Factors to Consider Before Creating or Purchasing Your Survival Kit

As already discussed, there is no survival kit that could possibly prepare you for every conceivable tragedy. Even the best ones can't cover the staggering number of variables operating in the natural world. Attempting to compensate for all the "what ifs" in the wilderness would 1) terrify you, and 2) require gear that weighed several hundred pounds. Therefore, it makes sense to look at what has statistically killed the majority of outdoor enthusiasts.

As learned in chapter 8, statistics show that the number-one outdoor killer is death by exposure, either through hypothermia or hyperthermia. Statistics also attest that it is the weather that dishes out the majority of punishment and misery and contributes greatly to the overall success of any wilderness SAR mission. Therefore, the most important survival kit components should be those that directly or indirectly regulate core body temperature. While Mother Nature can deliver an arsenal of "what ifs," she is also very simple and basic, and, in the end, simplicity always wins. Remember, the outdoors is neutral, she is neither for you nor against you. She just is. It's our job to adapt to whatever face she puts on at the time.

Preparing Your Kit: 13 Tantalizing, Tried-and-True Tips to Follow Before Creating Your Emergency Stash

The following list of factors should be reviewed before you attack the concept of what to pack in your setup. Regardless of who you are and what your intentions may be, you'll find the following concepts helpful in deciding what and how to pack for greater effectiveness in almost any environment. The more we address these common variables in preparing an effective wilderness survival kit, the more obvious it becomes that the kit is not just for wilderness survival.

Our urban, civilized world is arguably the most dependent culture on the planet, which is a side effect from decades of not taking responsibility for our lives. The more rules, regulations, lawsuits, and insurance the nation takes on, the flabbier our self-reliance muscles become. In our technological cosmology, as awesome as it is, we have become slaves to the system itself, not knowing quite what to do if the bottom falls out. At the end of a long day of doing something they hate, most Americans drive home to their 30-year mortgage shelters. Once there, they obtain water and food from holes located within its walls. They cook the food and heat or cool the shelter from a magic source originating from God-knows-where, and they don't give it a second thought. Only when these luxuries get cut off during a civil emergency or power outage does reality set in. Make no mistake, the benefits of a well-thought out survival kit will shine just as brightly from your backyard as they do in the wilderness. Taking responsibility for yourself and your loved ones is just good ol' common sense. Don't get caught with your pants down by assuming that someone else will take care of your problems, whether you're at home or in the wilderness.

Prepare Your Kit to Be:

1. Relevant to the environment encountered.
2. Lightweight and portable.
3. Waterproof.
4. Durable and dependable.
5. Complementary to the physical fitness and expertise levels of the user.
6. Able to meet a wide variety of conditions—back to basics.
7. Comprised of multiple-use components.
8. Comprised of calorie-conserving components.
9. Panic-proofed—containing components that can be utilized if you are injured.
10. Comprised of components that can be easily purchased or made.
11. Affordable yet effective.
12. Field-tested—use it or lose it!
13. *Simple!*

Relevant to the Environment

In Arizona, creating a survival kit that's relevant to the environment encountered is a challenge because Arizona has more geographical diversity in the shortest drive time of any region in North or South America. I can drive from Phoenix in the Sonoran Desert, to the town of Flagstaff near the San Francisco Mountains with their alpine tundra in less than 3.5 hours. In that time, I'll pass through 10 different vegetation life zones, which is the equivalent of driving from Mexico to Canada. As a result, it's possible to be faced with a desert or winter-survival scenario within the same day. Even with this geographical challenge, if you stick to the basics of regulating body temperature, your kit should need little modification from region to region. Research the area you'll be traveling in for specific information that might make or break your experience and pack your kit accordingly. An excursion into the wilderness of Alaska will have different needs than a backcountry trip to Mexico.

Lightweight and Portable

If your kit's not lightweight and portable, you're not going to carry it with you. Instead it will be collecting dust in the back of your closet or under the truck seat. A survival kit shouldn't weigh 30 pounds or more or be a drag to lug around. It should be composed of the simplest methods available for preserving your life. Strive to design your kit with as little volume and weight as is practical. For example, the items in my kit weigh a hair over four pounds. The less obtrusive it is, the more likely it'll be on your person when you need it.

Waterproof

There's at least one item that should always be waterproof in your kit. Can you guess what it is? Yup, your matches. Some environments demand that you waterproof the entire enchilada. Again, knowing as much as you can about the area you're heading into will save you a lot of grief. If your trip research points to the fact that your destination will be dry, don't assume it will be. In this age of plastic barriers galore, there's little excuse for not having some way of keeping your kit and body dry.

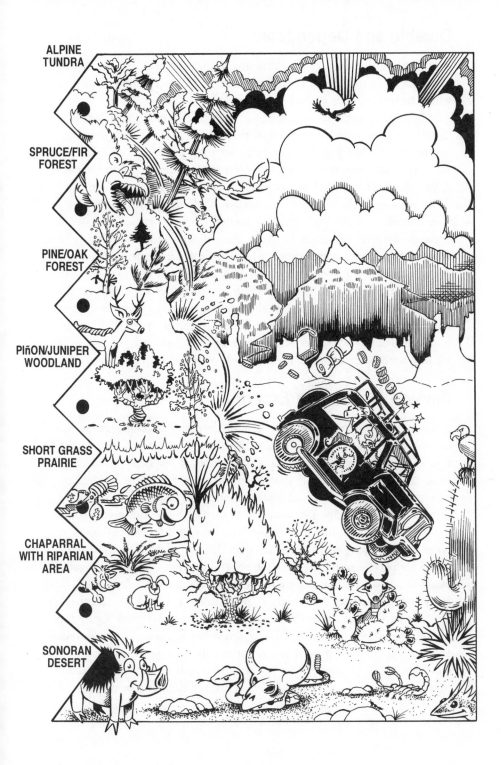

ALPINE TUNDRA

SPRUCE/FIR FOREST

PINE/OAK FOREST

PIñON/JUNIPER WOODLAND

SHORT GRASS PRAIRIE

CHAPARRAL WITH RIPARIAN AREA

SONORAN DESERT

Durable and Dependable

If your kit is not durable and dependable, prepare your gene pool to have one less participant. This is your survival kit—it's not a place you want cheaply made gear that won't hold up to abuse.

My kit recently went through a heinous test of durability. I was meeting a news crew from Ohio in the desert for a two-day shoot on survival skills. My Jeep blew a clutch so a friend offered to drive. As we were loading his truck, I foolishly left my kit sitting next to the passenger door. He backed out of the driveway, turned the wheel, and drove right over the top of it. Awesome! While this is not something I would have carried out myself, I savored the experience as I went through the bundle, piece by piece, to see what had survived. The weight of the truck blew open my bottle of iodine, shattered my compass, and flattened the film vial carrying my tinder, but that was all. Amazing! Incidentally, one of my quart water bottles took a direct hit from the front tire and, other than inflicting minor scratches, was unharmed. I can't help but think it was saved by the two rows of duct tape wrapped around its middle. While you might not run over your survival kit with a truck, carrying quality gear will pay you back many times over.

Physical Fitness and Expertise

A point that's completely overlooked in commercial kits is making the kit complementary to the physical fitness and expertise levels of the user. Human beings have dramatic differences in levels of physical fitness, ability, and agility. If you weigh 400 pounds, have bad knees, severe asthma, or are a couch potato in general, you'll need to modify things—and that's OK. I'm simply hammering home the myth of the one-size-fits-all kit. In any survival scenario, your physical body is what you're trying to take home, sans the body bag. Obviously, the better shape you're in, the more stress you can place upon your vehicle. If you had a Pinto compete in the Indy 500, it wouldn't do so well. How can you expect your body to place much better if it's old, tired, and out of shape? While I'm not Richard Simmons (thank God) the importance of physical fitness during stress situations can't be ignored. Practice using your kit until you're intimately aware of how to use its contents. While you might not be an expert, as if there is such a thing in the woods, your kit should reflect whatever skill level you're at.

The Kit

⇧ This eyeglass-case-sized pouch holds the majority of my survival-kit components. There's no excuse not to carry this gear!

⇧ My nemesis: A bevy of commercial survival kits.

The whole enchilada! ⇩

C-1

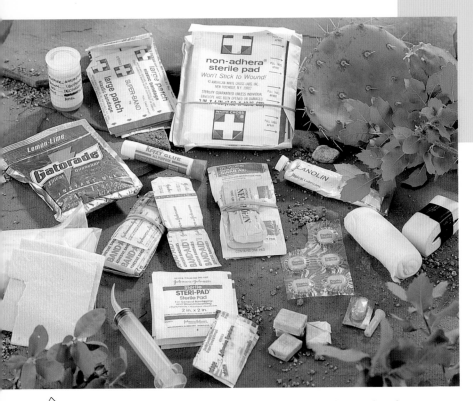

⬆ **The bowels of my homemade first-aid kit.**

Two mini-kits. Notice the whistle and small LED light. ⬇

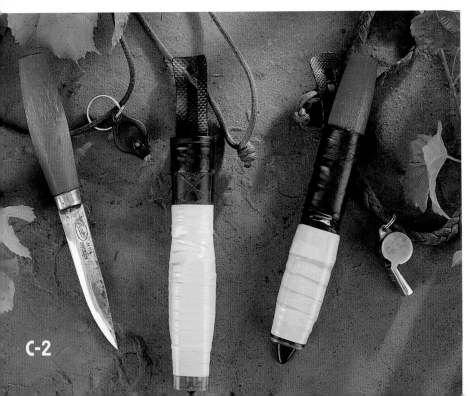

Fire

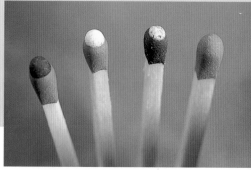

A plethora of commercially available matches. Notice the extreme differences in their sizes.

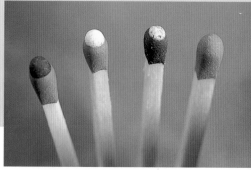
Matches (from left to right): new wooden, strike-anywhere kitchen match; the same but with different-colored head; old (several years) strike-anywhere kitchen match (notice that the white tip has noticeably faded when compared to the other); wooden, "strike-on-the-box" kitchen match (notice that the match head is all one color).

A split, wooden, strike-anywhere kitchen match and a split paper match each provide two chances to light a fire. POWs during WW II split wooden matches up to six times!

Commercial and improvised match safes. The ridiculous, army-green-colored one can be brightly taped as suggested at the bottom. The match safe on the far right sucks big time and should be avoided at all costs. Notice improvised striking surfaces.

The proper way to strike a match. Use your middle finger to support the match head while striking so it won't break.

Waxed, "strike-anywhere" kitchen matches, loaded and ready to go in a quality, highly visible match safe. Notice the sandpaper striking surface rubber-cemented to the cap.

The painfully obvious difference between an adjustable lighter and a non-adjustable. Which one would you rather use to make a fire?

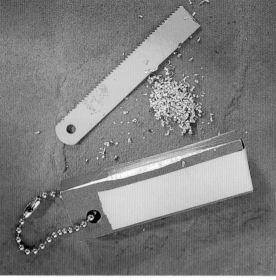

The magnesium block with striking insert. The yellow tape and yellow hacksaw blade help with visibility.

A pile of magnesium shavings created by using the end of the yellow hacksaw blade to scrape away at the block. Notice shiny area on block from scraping.

The Pink Floyd majesty of burning magnesium, 5,400 degrees strong. Who needs drugs!?

Various types and sizes of metal matches (mish-metal). Check out the massive size of a couple of them when compared to the mish-metal striking insert in the yellow magnesium block.

The Potency of Homemade Tinder

↑ Tearing open a petroleum-jelly saturated cotton ball to expose the inner target area.

⇒ Scraping a mish-metal insert into the "dry" target area of the ball. ⇒

⬇ The all-powerful tinder bundle, in this case made from juniper bark. Left: Virgin juniper bark. Bottom three piles consist of fine, medium, and coarse pieces of bark. The completed tinder bundle is at the top.

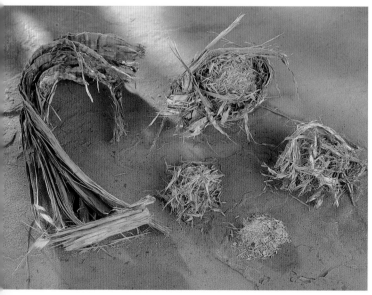

↑ Igniting a tinder bundle with a mish-metal striking insert.

Cotton ball has been burning for 15 seconds. ⟹ Burning for 2½ minutes. ⟹ Burning for more than 4 minutes.

⟸

Blowing a tinder bundle into flame with 16 percent exhaled oxygen from my lungs.

⟹

Smoldering tinder bundle. A well-made tinder bundle of this size can smolder for half an hour in windless conditions. Want flame? Just blow.

C-7

Using a Fresnel Lens

Backing off the lens from the target to make the full circle of light as pinpoint as possible. Notice wisp of smoke that should appear within seconds.

⬆ Making a "half circle" of light. ⇒ Rotating the lens to create a "full circle" of light. ⇒

⬇ Using a Fresnel lens to create an ember in a tinder bundle.

⬆ Constructing a typical, cone-shaped fire lay. Notice the target area of fine stuff in the center. Your heat or ignition source will be placed under this.

Shelter

Garbage-bag raincoat. Although you'll look like a giant Hershey's kiss, putting the face hole in this position keeps rain and wind off the head and neck while the other "corner" allows space to carry and keep dry a small day pack.

Improvised tube tent made from two 55-gallon barrel liners.

↑ Quality, commercial space blankets. Notice the highly visible, bright-orange backing on the larger heavy-duty model.

↑ Homemade corner grommets made from duct tape and safety pins on a regular-sized space blanket.

Water

↑ Using a drinking tube to gather water from a rock crevice.

↰ Gathering water with a freezer bag from a pool in a God-forsaken, mosquito-infested swamp.

A quart- and gallon-sized heavy-duty freezer bag loaded with water. The zipper seal of the gallon-sized bag (right) is supporting more than eight pounds of weight!

Future emergency water containers: Jumbo-size, non-lubricated condoms.

Carrying the goods "hobo style" in an extra bandana.

Nearly a gallon of water in a condom.

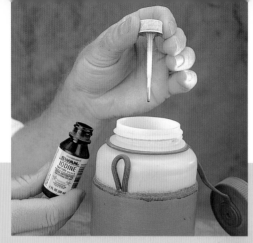

Disinfecting, drop by drop, one U.S. quart of water with—your friend and mine—tincture of Iodine 2 percent.

Signaling

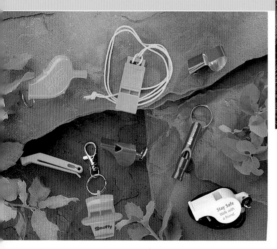

The "front" side of commercial and homemade signal mirrors. The 3 x 5 glass sweetheart in the upper left-hand corner is my baby.

The back side of the same mirrors. Notice that the mirror I carry is only reflective on one side.

A ton of whistles. I prefer the bright orange, pea-less, flat version such as the one with the yellow lanyard. The blue beauty in the upper right-hand corner is made from a strip of aluminum, a Mors Kochanski classic.

Using a
sightable
signal mirror.

Colored surveyor's tape used as a cross-country flag. A permanent marker can be used to write a note to your rescuers on the tape.

The tin-foil tip-off manifest. All it needs now, if you are in a group of people, is your name written in the corner.

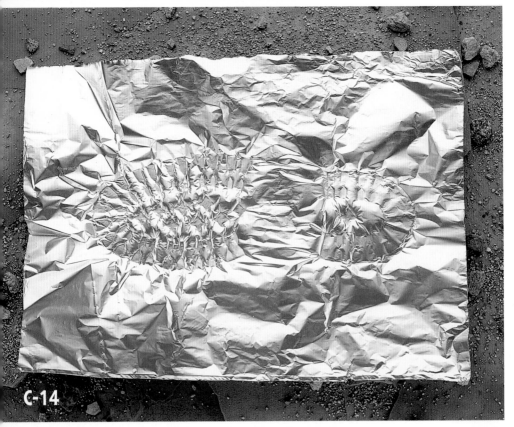

Other Goodies
Cutting Down a Small Willow with My Knife

⬆ Starting the blade at a 45-degree angle while slightly bending the tree.

⬆ Finishing the cut by bending the tree and pushing down hard on the knife while rocking the blade back and forth.

⟹

Total time: Three seconds. Yee-ha! The cut willow can be used in dozens of wilderness applications, from making shelter, to spears, to quickie bows, and more.

Test for hypothermia and dexterity. If you can't easily touch your little finger to your thumb, stop what you're doing and get warm!

The difference between true, seven-strand parachute cord (left) and the imposter called "paracord."

Removing a little bit of heaven—duct tape! Notice the super-handy parachute-cord loop.

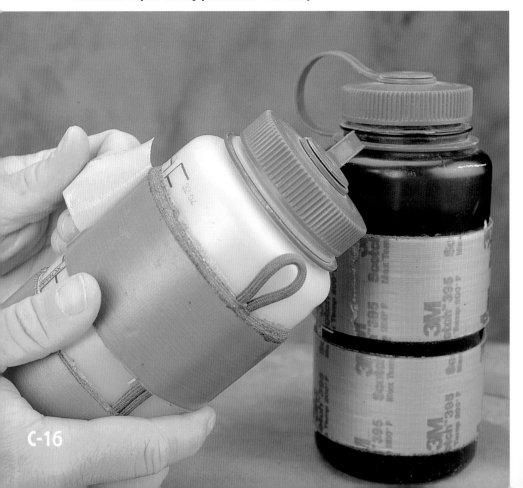

Variety of Conditions

For optimal adaptation in the field, your kit should meet a wide variety of conditions. Focusing on the basics allows for carrying less while improving options. Options are empowering as they provide choices. Choices allow you to pursue the best plan available at the time. Specialized gear, although it has its place, limits options for the survivor. You may find that a specialty item might perform one thing so well that it's worth carting along—the choice is yours.

Multiple-Use Components

Quality, multiple-use components are worth their weight in gold. Don't pack anything that has less than two uses and hopefully more. There are two master, multiuse components with which civilizations were built. Either one in the hands of a competent user can produce tremendous benefits, but either one in the hands of a loser can cause unprecedented pain, injury, and death. Can you guess what two goodies I'm talking about? They are a cutting edge and fire. Both have been around since time began and are each the epitomes of multiuse magic, accomplishing a plethora of tasks but taking up a minimal amount of space and weight.

COOL!!!

Desperate gear manufacturers have gone overboard trying to impress the population with a multitude of gidgets and gadgets. I've seen several multi-tools on the market and remain unimpressed. Some sprout so many contraptions that they are virtually functionless. Others have elements that refuse to work in the aisle of the discount store, let alone in the backcountry. If you need help extracting an emergency hangnail or getting a closer look at phone numbers in your little black book, they may be of some service. Don't let your quest for sound, multiple-use gear lead you into a land of cheesy, made-in-Hong Kong trash.

Calorie-Conserving Concepts

The energy stored within your body is one of the most sacred commodities you have in the backcountry. How much juice you have at the time of impending doom is determined by your physical fitness and attitude, prior activity level, environmental temperature extremes and clothing choices, the amount and type of food last eaten, your hydration level, and your level of fatigue. Energy can be intelligently conserved to last several days or be ignorantly wasted in a few hours depending on your state of mind, body shelter, and activity level.

Your body is like a battery as it stores only so much energy (calories) before it needs refueling. The chance that your "battery" will be full at the start of a survival scenario is about as likely as an honest politician working for the common good of all people—possible but not likely. Anything done to slow down calorie consumption, or achieve better efficiency from the ones you do burn, can increase your overall survival time. Calmly using the glucose in your brain by carefully thinking out plans and actions before you move your body saves a considerable amount of energy. Prioritize your situation to determine the most important actions necessary to get you rescued as quickly as possible. Spending extra energy traveling to a sheltered location or improvising protective shelter from the environment can save an enormous amount of calories and water that your body would have otherwise spent trying to keep warm (shivering) or cool (sweating). Your ultimate challenge and dilemma, using the tips from the right, is deciding how calories will be spent in order to get the greatest bang for your buck.

Calorie-Conserving Components

Every time you move, you're accelerating the loss of calories and water, two very precious commodities in the backcountry. Packing and using calorie-conserving components gets the job done with a minimum of athletics. Guys love hearing this, but you want to be as lazy as possible in your emergency situation while still getting your needs met. If your compromising event becomes long-term, you'll be glad you conserved all the energy you could from the onset. History is full of survival scenarios in which those involved took for granted they would be rescued right away and willfully pissed away all of their supplies in the beginning. Some of them lived to tell the story, others . . . well, you get the picture.

1. *Stay comfortable*. Regulating body temperature from the start by adding or subtracting layers when needed is one of the easiest and most effective methods to conserve energy. Critical body areas to protect are the core and head and neck.
2. *Slow down*. Working at 60 percent of your maximum output allows the body to burn stored fat instead of limited carbohydrate reserves.
3. *Prioritize and plan tasks in your mind*. It requires a lot less energy to think about doing something than it does to do it.
4. *Don't sweat*. Unless the weather is hot, sweating is your body's way of saying that you're doing too much too fast. Sweating is the body's response to burning huge amounts of metabolic calories and further dehydrates the body.
5. *Stay dry in cold weather*. Wet clothing robs the body of precious heat energy.
6. *Don't freak out*. Panicked and fearful people compromise their survival in several ways, including spending energy running around like chickens with their heads cut off.
7. *Take rest breaks*. Resting reduces your energy output, increases morale, breaks up periods of boredom, allows muscles to rid themselves of lactic acid build up from exertion, and helps the body recover from fatigue. Don't forget the benefits of the all-powerful catnap talked about earlier.
8. *Graze*. Eating small amounts of food throughout the day, especially simple carbohydrates, provides energy while allowing the body to access fat reserves for metabolism.
9. *Stay hydrated*. If possible, drink warmed fluid in cold weather and cool fluids in hot weather to hydrate the body without sacrificing calories to heat up or cool down the water internally.

Panic Proofed

Since accidents comprise a large percentage of how a person gets screwed, kit components should be panic-proofed and contain components that can be utilized if you are injured. Injuries are extremely common. The bummed-up knee, the sprained ankle, the nasty wound—all can be major bummers and severely restrict the ability to operate gear. Could you use your knife left-handed if your right gets mashed between rocks? Can you construct a shelter from emergency gear with a strained ligament? The fewer bells and whistles gear has, the easier it'll be to use under the strain and stress of painful injuries. Again, sticking to basics helps increase your odds for success.

Panic greatly reduces your chances for survival. It also renders fine and complex motor skills useless. Striking the match in your backyard was easy, but when you are consumed with fear, the task becomes monumental. Packing gear that involves fine- or complex-motor-skill movements is a big mistake. I'm not saying don't pack matches, but have a gross-motor movement alternative just in case, such as a road flare or magnesium block with striking insert. Simple, gross-motor functions are far easier to perform under stress than fine- and complex-motor functions. This has been proven in combat situations for decades. Keep gear and how you use it simple.

Easily Purchased or Made

Some particulars need to be changed or rotated for maximal effectiveness as they rust, wear out, become frayed, brittle, or outdated. Using components that can be easily purchased or made allows for acquiring new items with less hassle. I have received several notes from people offering suggestions regarding what I carry. Many are good ideas but involve specialty-shop items that are hard to come by for the average person. Pack simple yet effective gear that is widely available. Replacing the bulb in your specialty flashlight is a pain in the neck if you're not near the store you bought it from. Add in human nature and procrastination and you might realize that you forgot to score that new bulb when it's dusk and you're 10 miles down a trail with a torn tendon.

The advantage of being able to make items yourself from everyday materials is a major plus. Creating gear yourself gives you an intimate, up-close perspective on what you'll be carrying. This allows you to modify certain traits of the item at will, thereby better serving your needs. Best of all, it's hard to imagine a homemade piece of gear that its creator doesn't know how to use well. If you're into specialty gear, that's fine, but order a couple extras so you won't have to hassle with restocking for a while.

Affordable Yet Effective

Quality components that meet the majority of your needs don't have to drive you into the poorhouse but can be affordable yet effective. I've been called cheap by more than one person. It's such a harsh word. I prefer thrifty. But I must admit, if there is an alternative that's less expensive, I've explored it. I don't mind paying good money for righteous gear, but you'll find you don't need to spend an arm and a leg for an effective kit, unless you're hanging out deep within the Amazon jungle. Another advantage of compiling your own kit is the luxury of price shopping. The advantages of homemade components speak for themselves when it comes to saving money. Cost aside, spend what you need to, as it's a life-insurance plan that will pay for itself handsomely if you have to collect on the policy.

Field Tested

Your kit must be field-tested—use it or lose it. Ideally, you should completely wear out the contents by practicing how they're used. Experiment with what you pack! Explore each item's advantages and disadvantages now, long before the emergency arrives. Owning a survival kit that you haven't used is like reading a book on how to swim when the boat's going down. Practice on duplicate gear so the stuff you carry is 100 percent new and ready to go, not worn out and battered. Yes, it will cost you twice as much money, but aren't you and your loved ones worth it?

Simple

The concept of keeping it simple is arguably the most important. It is the glue that holds everything together. It's the master concept in which all things should be contained. Your trip planning, your gear, the survival kit you carry, the game plan you leave with your two trusted people—everything should be simple. Simplicity is the key to life and certainly to any panic situation. Don't underestimate this powerful force; keep it simple!

SURVIVAL KIT COMPONENTS

YOU
+ THE TOOL
+ THE ENVIRONMENT

= YOUR LIFE

In general, I pack the following items in my kit, but as I mentioned earlier, people's needs are different. I'm not you, and vice versa, and we won't be there to sing "Kumbayah" to each other if the ship goes down. High grade what you want from my list, add what you want from yours, and scrap the rest. I modify kits as necessary, depending on geographical life zones, weather factors, the number of people in my group, terrain issues, the accessibility of the area to rescue teams, or whatever other factors I feel are important.

Don't let your kit become a static lump that never sees the light of day until it's needed. I'm constantly dinking around, replacing this, repairing that, adding something here, or taking something out. Certain core items, however, have remained intact for several years. I won't replace matches with something else anytime soon, if ever, and some elements are so basic to regulating body temperature or signaling for rescue that they have become crucial. Their importance in helping us survive will be around as long as the physical laws that govern this planet. Next to each item in the list, I've included its weight in ounces.

My Kit Components List

Kit Item	Weight in ounces	Discussed on page
• *Two heavy-duty freezer bags (gallon and quart size)*	$1/2$	137
• *Tincture of iodine 2%*	1	138
• *Condom (nonlubricated)*	$1/8$	142
• *Regular space blanket (bronze-and silver-sided type)*	2	144
• *One roll dental floss*	$1/4$	146
• *Colored surveyor's tape (3 or 4 feet)*	$1/2$	147
• *Pea-less brightly colored plastic whistle*	$1/8$	149
• *Paraffin-coated, strike-anywhere kitchen matches in brightly colored match safe*	1	150
• *Disposable butane lighter (brightly colored, nonopaque, adjustable flame, nonchild-proof)*	$1/2$	157
• *Magnesium-block fire starter with hacksaw-blade striker*	$1 1/2$	161
• *6 to 8 cotton balls saturated with petroleum jelly in brightly colored film vial*	1	166
• *Credit-card-sized magnifying lens in brightly colored sheath*	$1/4$	168
• *Flashlight and lanyard with two AA batteries (brightly colored)*	4	170
• *Two AA batteries with date of purchase*	2	171
• *Extra carbon-steel knife with sheath*	4	172
• Clear plastic drinking tube, 3 feet long	1	178
• Collapsible, 1- to 2-gallon water container	$1/2$	179
• Two 55-gallon barrel liners or three large-capacity leaf bags (store rolled up in gallon freezer bag)	6	180
• Heavy-duty space blanket (brightly colored)	12	182
• Wool or synthetic stocking cap (brightly colored)	$2 1/2$	183
• Cotton bandana (brightly colored)	1	184
• 100 feet of 550-pound-test parachute cord (white for summer, olive for winter)	4	185
• 3 x 5-inch glass, sightable signal mirror with brightly colored duct-tape-reinforced pouch	5	187
• Homemade first-aid kit	10	191
• Uncle Peppy's patented power pack stack	$1/8$	194
• 7.5 minute topographical map and compass	2	198
• Two candy or nutrition bars	$4 1/8$	201
Total weight =	66.8 oz. or 4.2 lbs.	

My Survival Kit Container

Although this seems like a lot of gear, the *italicized* items fit into a pouch the size of an eyeglass case. I carry my survival kit in a large-capacity fanny pack. I've arranged items to take up as little space as possible, thereby using most of the pack for food, instructional materials for students, or extra clothes. I don't like things hanging from my shoulders, so I rarely use backpacks. I take my fanny pack into the bush 90 percent of the time. Because of this, I need all the extra space I can get.

Attached to my fanny pack's waist belt, I carry two, one-quart water bottles, one on either side to evenly distribute the weight in my pack. Two bottles make disinfecting water with halogens easier and give me a second chance if I lose or break a bottle. Both bottles feature a wide mouth, making it easier to collect and disinfect water for drinking. This also makes it less of a hassle if the contents freeze.

On the eighth day, the Lord created duct tape. This sticky stuff holds a special place in my heart because its uses are virtually limitless.

Wide Mouth "Unbreakable" Plastic Bottle

Parachute Cord Loop

Duct Tape

Upon two areas of each bottle I've applied as much duct tape as possible while still allowing it to fit within its carrying pouch. One bottle has professional-grade duct tape from the hardware store that touts a 212°F (100°C) delamination rating. When purchasing tape, most larger hardware stores give you three choices in regard to quality. I've labeled them "I wish I were a man", "I think I'm a man," and "By God, I am a man." (As thrifty as I can be, I buck up and gleefully fork over the extra dough to have within my presence this wonderfully sticky salvation.) My other bottle sports "100 mile-an-hour" military tape that incorporates a tensile strength of 45 pounds per inch and an adhesion rating of 55 ounces per inch with the bonus of a 10-percent stretch factor. The tape gets its name from the military, which once used it to temporarily repair bullet holes in airplanes. Its delamination rating, however, is only 150°F (65°C). Apply the tape carefully, wrapping it on top of itself until you reach the desired thickness. Take the old tape off and add new stuff every year to year and a half, depending on how beat up or delaminated it looks.

One of my bottles has a short piece of parachute cord inserted under the tape. The top of the cord forms a loop that allows me to tie on cordage and lower the bottle into a crevice, wash, or windmill casing to retrieve water. The loop enables me to easily carry the bottle from a shoulder sling or other improvised method, thereby freeing up my hands to accomplish more important tasks. On extended desert trips, I carry more water or make caches in key areas before the journey.

Attached to the outside of my fanny pack, I carry an extra flashlight and a multi-tool. Aaaauugghh! Yes, I said multi-tool. I've been carrying one for more than nine years, yet have used it only two or three times. The main reason I carry one at all is for the wire cutters; the world is full of old, rusty barbed-wire fencing, and real fencing tools are extremely heavy. If you're a pilot or are into firearms or other technical doodads, multi-tools are nice, but be sure to purchase a quality pair.

The external flashlight is my principal light because it's easier to find than the one buried within my pack. I carry two since I work with students in the backcountry and frequently visit deserts where high temperatures require nighttime travel. My fanny pack, like most, sports an array of bungee cords and tie straps that are capable of anchoring other gear if needed.

What you use as a kit container is up to you. It could be a coffee can, soap dish, fishing vest, belt pack, fanny pack, or whatever containment system fits your intention and lifestyle. Use something detachable from the bigger picture so you can carry it alone if necessary. In other words, if your kit's located within a compartment of a large-capacity backpack, the odds of you being too lazy to put its contents into something more manageable for a short hike skyrocket.

Survival Kit Priorities

In your enthusiasm to escape to the nearest trailhead, don't forget what your kit is supposed to accomplish. Its main focus is to regulate core body temperature and allow you to signal for rescue, while conserving what energy you have and improve your situation. In our three-day, 72-hour scenario, everything else carried is statistically fluff.

Even a first-aid kit, while exceptional in its value, should take a backseat to the above. Although the art of pre-hospital emergency medicine began more than 30 years ago in the United States, many variables exist in the wilderness. To cover them all medically or otherwise would require a large-capacity backpack and more. Most people enjoying the backcountry are not physicians, and many lack basic first-aid and CPR training. In fact, 95 percent of all rescues are performed without the aid of a physician, relying instead on first responders, emergency medical technicians (EMTs), and paramedics who may or may not have training in wilderness medicine and rescue techniques. Everyone on the planet should receive at least basic first-aid and CPR instruction, especially those wishing to pursue quality time in the outdoors. Folks who practice wilderness medicine know that with the exception of certain drugs and neat techniques, all they're hoping to do is stabilize the patient in order to transport them to a real medical facility. This same drama has been played out on wartime battlefields for decades.

If you have a major problem in the field with the A, B, Cs (airway, breathing, and circulation), you're in big trouble. If a medical emergency is going to take you out, you probably won't have the training, help, or equipment on site to deal with it, especially if you're the typical outdoor enthusiast. Am I saying blow off the first-aid kit? Absolutely not!

Explaining My Kit Components

I'll explain each item starting at the top of the list, including where to find it or how to make it, why it's carried, and a little on how it's used. *Truly knowing how to use the contents is your responsibility.* This knowledge cannot be learned from a book, a video, or from a lot of wishing. Cowboy up, get off your butt, and figure out how the gear you're choosing to shluck around works. Again, don't whip out the "how-to-swim" book when the boat's going down.

HEAVY DUTY

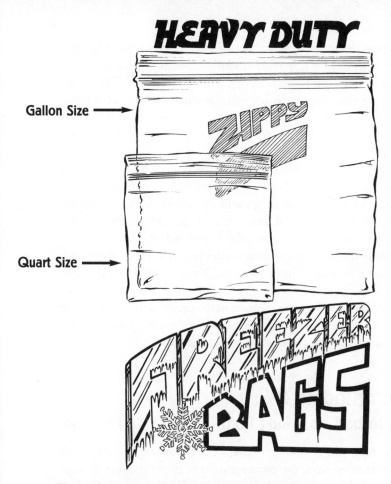

Gallon Size ⟶

Quart Size ⟶

ZIPPY

FRESH BAGS

Two heavy-duty freezer bags (one gallon and one quart):
Courageous, cheap containment for a plethora of precarious predicaments.

Containers are incredibly valuable in the bush. They are an art form. In the woods, you need to know how to make pottery, weave a basket, use fire to hollow out wood, grow gourds, have access to animal parts, or be hip to some other method in order to achieve containment. Entire cultures evolved around container use; ask any hunter-gatherer tribe.

Freezer bags are tough, cheap, commonly available containers, and their uses are only limited by your imagination. These are collapsible containers that can fit virtually anywhere. Conveniently enough, gallon-sized bags will hold a gallon of water while quart sizes hold a quart. Brand-name freezer bags have quality zipper seals that if treated gently, will support the water weight of a filled bag without popping open.

Freezer bags have a very wide "mouth." Compare it to the mouth of a traditional water bottle and the bag wins hands down. This mouth is wonderful for scooping up water, especially in road ruts, as it allows you to skim the top of a puddle while minimally disturbing the muddy bottom. Practice will enable you to achieve a surprising volume of water in one scoop.

Many nooks and crannies in the backcountry hold water that can't be reached using a regular-sized water bottle. If water has pooled between rocks or other unyielding surfaces, however, the freezer bag can be compressed in the hand, lowered into the crevice, and filled. If you can get your hand into an area, the baggie will follow.

Use common sense when storing freezer bags and rotate them every year since plastic becomes brittle over time. Keep in mind that the more folds and creases you put into a bag, trying to make it as small as possible, the more weak spots you're creating in the plastic. Last but not least, purchase brand-name freezer bags. Cheap store-name brands are just that—there is a difference in quality; spend the extra 65 cents—you're worth it.

Tincture of Iodine 2%:
How not to barf up a lung from the faucet to the field.

Water in the field can be contaminated by organic and inorganic substances from land erosion, the disintegration of minerals, rotting vegetation, earth- and water-borne biological cooties, industrial chemical pollutants, and microorganisms from animal and human waste. This last nasty is the biggest concern for most outdoor travelers.

There are several ways to disinfect water. "Water disinfection" means killing or removing the pathogens or bugs that make us ill. While its usage is technically associated with chemical halogens such as iodine and chlorine, it can be applied to filtration and heat as well. "Water purification" involves the removal of organic and inorganic chemicals and particulate matter that deal with how water looks, tastes, and smells. It has nothing to do with the art of eliminating harmful microorganisms. For our purposes, how the wet stuff looks, tastes, and otherwise isn't nearly as important as how not to barf up a lung while filling your pants with excrement. Severe diarrhea can increase fluid loss at a horrifying rate, up to 25 quarts in a 24-hour period! Water disinfection is a huge subject and can be somewhat complex, so I won't go into the many other methods in this book.

There are four families of critters that cause us grief: protozoa, parasites, bacteria, and viruses. Some of these creatures pack a serious punch and can make you dead if they are not dealt with. It's estimated that 1.5 billion rural people and 200 million urban folks in our world suffer from poor sanitation and the lack of safe drinking water. Worldwide, 28,000 to 68,000 people die each day from diseases caused by contaminated water and unhealthy conditions. Iodine kills every one of the little bastards with the exception of the protozoa *Cryptosporidium parvum*, which infects many herd animals, including cows, goats, sheep, deer, and elk.

Aside from heat, chemical disinfection is the primary method used for treating water in the backcountry. Iodine is a chemical halogen available in many forms, including 5 percent to 7 percent solution, 10 percent solution, tablets, crystals, and 2 percent tincture. Regardless of what form you choose, it must remain in contact with the water for a certain period of time in order for it to do its killing. The amount of contact time required varies in regard to the water's temperature and pH, how strong the iodine solution was made, the type of microorganisms that are present, and the quantity of nitrogen compounds and particulate matter found within the water.

The wilderness areas I travel in are subject to cattle, dogs, people, beaver, and plenty of other known carriers of various waterborne pathogens. In general, I use five drops of tincture of iodine 2 percent per quart of water, although as many as 10 drops may be used. For most of the water sources I frequent, I let the five drops sit for 30 minutes. If this is the case, then you can bet your butt the water I've treated was *clear* and *temperate*. This is important as water temperature and clarity affect how long iodine needs to sit before the water is safe to drink. Turbidity, or a water's "cloudiness," is caused by suspended particulate matter such as clay, silt, plankton, and other microscopic organisms, and is often the culprit behind water that tastes and smells crappy. Funky-looking surface water is a common occurrence in the backcountry and contains 10 times the organic carbon content of aquifer groundwater. Waterborne pathogens can absorb into or already be imbedded within the floating matter to such an extent that organisms in the center of the chunks are somewhat protected from disinfection methods. Iodine and chlorine are halogens. Both readily bond to nitrogen compounds, organic and inorganic, that are present within the water. These nitrogen compounds, commonly referred to as pond scum, mess with the halogen's ability to kill, requiring either more sit time for the water to disinfect or increased amounts of halogen. In the case of sodium hypochlorite 5.25 percent, otherwise known as chlorine bleach, organic

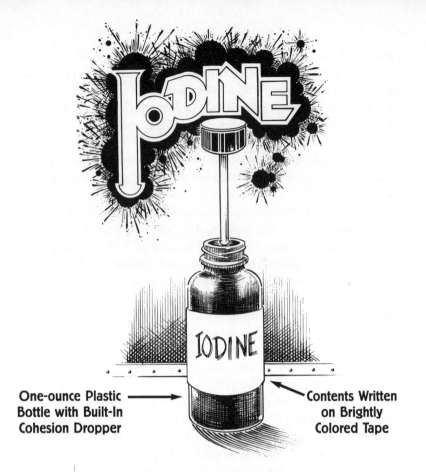

One-ounce Plastic Bottle with Built-In Cohesion Dropper

Contents Written on Brightly Colored Tape

matter bonds with the chlorine itself, and actually changes its chemical makeup into something called chloramine, which doesn't do jack to disinfect your water. This is just one reason why chlorine sucks for field-water disinfection.

Filtering out water turbidity decreases the number of microorganisms present in the first place, which decreases the amount of iodine needed to disinfect the water, thus making the water look and smell a whole lot better. Water clarity can be improved by simply letting the water sit or by straining it through a piece of clothing, bandana, or grass filter.

In general, iodine and halogens are very temperature sensitive and take longer to do their work when it's cold. Thus, the colder the water, the longer the contact time is needed in order to successfully eliminate bad bugs. For extremely cold water, let the five drops sit for two to three hours, or longer, if possible. To cut down on the sit time, you can also add more iodine, up to 10 drops per quart, although the water will again taste like doo-doo. Packing two or more bottles helps, as it allows you to treat one bottle while you drink the other.

Although impractical to execute in the field, water pH is also a factor. Halogens form several compounds, each with different disinfection rates, by oxidizing in water. How well each compound works is determined by pH. In general, the optimal pH for halogen disinfection is 6.5 to 7.5. The more alkaline the water, the greater the dose of iodine required. If water becomes extremely alkaline, as it does in some parts of my beloved desert, it's usually too nasty to drink anyway.

A word to the wise. If the water you score is pretty much funk city and difficult to filter, *add more iodine* rather than just prolonging the contact time. When dealing with extremely questionable liquid, both the color and the taste of iodine-treated water can be used as rough indicators for proper disinfection. In these circumstances, if the iodine taste created would gag a camel and the contents of your bottle appears yellow to light brown, you've successfully achieved 0.6 parts per million or greater, which is a good thing.

To summarize, strain the water if necessary to get rid of organic and inorganic matter, and then add no more than 10 drops of iodine per U.S. quart. Give the bottle a little shake. If the water is fairly temperate, let the solution sit for 30 minutes. Before drinking, partially unscrew the lid and turn the bottle upside down, allowing the treated water to dribble down the threads, as it only takes a drop to get ill. By the way, if you flavor water to make it more palatable and the flavoring contains vitamin C (ascorbic acid), it will neutralize the iodine (and its nasty taste!) before it does its duty. Wait 30 minutes or longer before adding the flavoring! Zinc brushes are also available to rid the water of its iodine taste. I'm not about to carry around this one-trick pony, but to each his or her own.

Another major advantage to carrying tincture of iodine 2 percent is its use as a topical wound disinfectant. When I was a kid, my skin was stained with iodine a good part of the time due to an assortment of scratches, cuts, abrasions, and punctures. This product allows you to disinfect your water and your wounds for less than a dollar—it's a screaming deal!

Tincture of iodine 2 percent has a much longer shelf life (up to several years longer) than compressed iodine tablets. It comes in its own unbreakable, one-ounce plastic bottle with a cohesion dropper and usually retails for under a buck. The bottle is typically tinted or opaque, giving the iodine greater protection from light sources. Circle the bottle with brightly colored tape for better visibility and write "Iodine" in permanent marker on its surface to minimize misunderstandings. It can be purchased at most discount pharmacies except

Wal-Mart; the "Greeting Gestapo" will kick you out of the store if you're barefoot. If the pharmacist doesn't have any in stock, they'll probably be able to order some. Make sure to purchase iodine that's "colored," since drops of the "denatured" or clear stuff are hard to see as they hit the water. This compact, lightweight, cheap, easily available, globally effective, multiuse, handy-to-use product with an extended shelf life is worth its weight in intestinal parasites for the outdoor enthusiast.

Warning! Check out any bottle of iodine at the neighborhood pharmacy and you'll spy a cute little skull and crossbones with the word "poison" written underneath. Telling the pharmacist what you wish to do with the tiny bottle will cause them to look at you funny and call store security. Truth be known, in the early 1900s, iodine was used to disinfect entire town water supplies. The Navy has performed gnarly, multimonth studies on unknowing ship-bound sailors in which extreme amounts of iodine were added to the ship's drinking water. So far, there have been no two-headed babies. Prisons, as well, have performed their patriotic duty by secretly experimenting on hundreds of inmates with no problems being reported. Regardless, iodine is recommended for short-term use only, no longer than 30 days. This is not a problem in the realm of our 3-day survival scenario. *Do not use iodine if you are pregnant, have a known allergy to iodine, or suffer from a thyroid problem.*

One condom (nonlubricated):
The private, passionate, pleasures of purchasing pompously portly prophylactics.

Water is a biological necessity down to the cellular level. It is not an optional item. In dry environments around the world, collapsible containers provide greater carrying capacity without the bulk of the container when not needed. Even in moist climates it's nice to have the option of transporting more of the wet stuff. An extra container allows for disinfecting greater quantities of water, permits "muddy" water to settle, limits frequent runs to the creek, and enables you to bask in the fact that you have a surplus of one of the survival world's most precious items. Heavy-duty, collapsible containers can be used as pillows or added ground insulation.

Although you should pack stronger collapsible water containers when possible, the humble condom does have its attributes. While offering reasonable protection from getting or giving the disease of the week, the condom does double-duty by saving your life in a far more unconventional fashion when it's used as an emergency water carrier.

Jumbo Size, Non-Lubricated

The best part about having a condom in your backcountry kit, whether you're male or female, is purchasing the little booger. Finally, men of all ages and backgrounds and the women who have suffered can say, with no uncertainty and in complete honesty, "I want the biggest, strongest condom you've got . . . nonlubricated, please." You'll be the envy of all your friends.

A condom containing a gallon of water is about the size of a volleyball. This extra gallon might grant you another day of life or more. I've filled condoms up to the size of watermelons, but if you so much as look at them wrong, they'll burst. Transport them hobo-style inside an extra bandana, shirtsleeve, or large sock, but use caution. As tough as condoms are, they're temperamental and can rupture at the most compromising times (as so many intimate couples can attest).

The trick to filling a condom is velocity. Filling one under a kitchen faucet is no problem due to the force of the water. But go to a static water source like a puddle or pond and it's another animal altogether. Unless the neck of the condom is sufficiently stretched out, the memory of the contracting rubber simply forces added water back out the mouth. Pre-stretching the neck before attempting to fill the beast increases your odds for success.

To fill, hold the condom's mouth open as wide as practical without destroying it. Using a brisk scooping motion, force as much water into the mouth as you can while trying not to drag the condom along the bottom of the water source. Another method is to hold the mouth open with one hand. This allows the other hand to use an improvised container, such as a hat or shoe, to pour water from a height, thereby producing water velocity to stretch the rubber. Once you've obtained a "globe" of water hanging from the stretched neck, you're free from fighting the self-emptying action of the little guy. Fun, isn't it? While using condoms containing spermicide and bizarre lubricants is doable in a pinch, it will cause even your closest friendships to suffer.

Like everything else in survival land, filling a condom is best practiced beforehand. Add it to your next party festivities, instead of bobbing for apples, for unique, good old-fashioned fun. Condoms can be purchased at a multitude of locations, including the truck-stop bathroom of your choice. Buy one with a brightly colored wrapper and replace it yearly. I have not yet tried a glow-in-the-dark model, but it may have some nighttime signaling advantages.

Regular space blanket (bronze and silver sided):
How to use that shiny thing you've had in the bottom of your pack since '87.

Space blankets are not truly blankets, as they have no dead-air space. They do, however, excel at reflecting radiant energy or heat from long- and short-wave radiation. Composed of aluminum-coated mylar plastic, the small, extremely shiny version supposedly reflects up to 80 percent of your body heat.

Space blankets have the power to reflect a fire's warmth toward you or blistering desert sun away from you, thus helping to regulate body temperature in virtually all climates. While not without its faults, this fact is a dream come true for the survival student.

In the cold, the easiest way to use one is to simply wrap it around your body, focusing on the core area. Reduce your body's surface area and increase its volume by huddling, thereby decreasing heat loss while preventing conduction from the ground. Use extreme caution, as space blankets don't breathe and are notorious vapor barriers. While they feel warm at first, over time trapped water vapor builds up on the inside of the blanket, which in turn soaks into clothing, destroying its insulating

space blanket

original BLANKET MADE IN USA

Silver- and Bronze-Sided Model

properties and hastening hypothermia. Hanging out the next night wearing ice, replacing what used to be dry insulation, is far from fun. Take great care to vent excess body moisture and avoid breathing into the blanket, as the breath gives off loads of water vapor.

In contrast, when it's hot enough to boil your brains, creatively pitched blankets function as a barrier against solar rays, producing life-saving shade that reflects the sun's damaging short-wave radiation.

I've experimented with scads of shelters built with these blankets. Some failed miserably while others worked great. When used as a reflector in combination with shelter and fire, space blankets kick butt. Suspend the blanket in whatever shape works so that you're sandwiched between it and the fire. The following story illustrates their usefulness.

During a winter-survival course in the Arizona high country, my students built two lean-to shelters with a fire in between. The shelters were made with downed timber, plastic, duct tape, and space blankets. That night, as the majority of us slept, the student on fire duty made the mistake of adding pitch wood to the blaze. This resin-saturated wood, common in dead conifer trees, burns like crazy and puts out an incredible amount of heat.

Before we hit the sack, I put up two thermometers. One hung from a fir tree several yards from camp, while the other was placed inside one of the shelters. The outside thermometer registered a nippy 15°F (-9°C). The one inside the shelter read a bone-melting 120°F (49°C)! Because of the increased heat from the burning pitch wood, students inside had stripped off all their clothing and their heads were sticking out from under the plastic to escape the oppressive temperature. The mistaken use of pitch wood nearly caused students to become hyperthermic during a winter-survival course. Such is the power of reflected and trapped radiation.

In full sun, space blankets make great signaling devices. While facing rescuers, unwrap the blanket and slowly flap it like you're shaking dust from of an old rug. This rolling motion creates a large surface area of reflective "movement and contrast" and looks like hundreds of tiny mirrors. Spend a few extra bucks and buy a blanket with a bronze-colored side, as it's much more visible when signaling on snow or large bodies of water.

Space blankets are not without sin, one of which is the extreme noise they create, especially in the wind. I don't dare break one out when I lecture or I have to yell over the racket while it's passed around the room. This is a small factor in a life-threatening situation, but keep it in mind so the noise doesn't drive you nuts. The aluminum coating is extremely thin and wears off easily. As soon as it's gone, your blanket no longer reflects heat and vaguely resembles the substance your cotton candy was wrapped in at the state fair. Even so, you'll still have a wind- and waterproof barrier, provided you don't rip it. Space blankets are as flimsy as our current civil liberties and tear quickly if manhandled. You can make grommets on the spot by duct taping the corners and attaching safety pins. Space blankets are also too small. If manufacturers would add a few more inches to each side, I might be able to use the damn thing without having to take a Yoga class beforehand.

All cons aside, this handy piece of gear reflects radiant heat, is lightweight, compact, easily accessible, cheap, and has multiple uses. Once opened, you'll need a Ph.D. in folding to get it back to its original size, so buy two, one to experiment with and the other to pack for the backcountry.

One roll of dental floss:
Four out of five dentists agree that you can easily afford this tiny but tough lightweight cord.

Dental floss is "rip-your-head-off" strong, easily available, cheap, small, lightweight, and multipurpose. I preach the merits of cordage later in the book, so I'll skip it here. Remove the actual spool of floss from its plastic container, which is bulky and serves little purpose other than

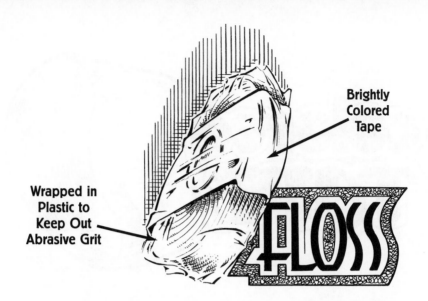

Brightly Colored Tape

Wrapped in Plastic to Keep Out Abrasive Grit

what it was intended for. Take the spool, typically only the size of a quarter yet composed of 100 feet of fiber, and cover it a few times with plastic wrap or the corner of a baggie to keep it clean. Grit and dust act like tiny knives and over time abrade the fibers in the cord, creating a weaker product. I carry good old-fashioned unwaxed floss. Get creative to fill your needs, as there are a lot of varieties on the market. Stay away from scented, minty assortments as they might attract unwanted fauna.

Colored surveyor's tape (3 or 4 feet):
An opportunity to play Hansel and Gretel without the mess.

Rolls of survey tape are available from your local hardware store. This nonsticky, stretchy, plastic tape comes in a variety of obnoxious colors that are perfect for visibility. It's widely used by Forest Service personnel and backcountry workers, so choose a color that's not commonly used in your area, as trees and bushes flagged with the same color of tape can cause confusion for rescuers. (This is the only reason I carry the orange variety over the yellow or other colors available.) Even so, UV rays from the sun wreak havoc on the tape, and break it down; thus it's not too difficult for searchers to discern fresh stuff from the older one hanging in the bush. If you write a note explaining your situation upon the tape itself and which direction you're headed, there will be even less confusion.

The rolls are quite large, so take a few feet off the mother roll and

colored TAPE

wrap it upon itself to form a little oval. The reason I carry survey tape is the "bread crumb" factor. If you need to proceed in a certain direction for whatever reason and find your way back, you can take small pieces of tape and pierce them at eye level upon objects ranging from saguaro cactus to spruce boughs.

To use, affix the first piece of tape at eye level upon the object of your choice, then proceed in your chosen direction of travel, turning ever so often to view the piece you last posted. When you're far enough away from the last piece, but can still see it, pick another tree, bush, stump, or rock pile and flag it. Make certain you can still witness the last piece of tape you used in the distance. Proceed in this manner, leapfrogging along, putting up new tape while still keeping within eye contact of the other. Don't make the distance between the pieces too far apart, as it's not hard to screw up and lose the last one, especially in dense brush or lighting changes caused by sun movement.

Using tape at eye level makes it easier to find. Even if a piece is temporarily lost on your return trip, a lot of up and down searching is eliminated, as you've put the tape on a specific plane in relation to your vision. Being able to proceed in a certain direction of travel and safely find your way back is an asset to any outdoor traveler. Using tape in questionable scenarios beforehand might prevent you from getting lost in the first place. Survey tape also doubles as weak cordage. With knowledge of the reverse-wrap, two-ply-cord method, it can be transformed into very strong cord. In another book, perhaps.

Pea-less, brightly colored plastic whistle:
When being a blow hard pays off.

Carry several ways to signal for rescue. Putting all of your eggs into one basket, like being at the mercy of direct sunlight with a signal mirror, can be frustrating at best and deadly at worst.

The ear-shattering decibels a whistle creates attract attention from a good distance while saving energy, body moisture, and your voice, and can be used to signal for help in any environment, in the midst of any temperature, elevation, or weather pattern. Although mountainous terrain, heavy woods, or even particulate matter in the air will muffle some of the whistle's punch, it is far more potent a sound signal than your screeching voice. People who have attended a heavy-metal concert know that they must carefully plan out their screaming or their vocal chords will become as impotent as a one-legged dog before three songs have passed.

Purchase a well-designed whistle that is plastic, pea-less, and painfully prominent in regard to its coloration. Plastic has less of a tendency to freeze to your lips during extreme cold weather, is lighter to carry, and is easy to find in traumatically bright, fluorescent colors. Older whistles relying on a cork or plastic "pea" whipping around a sound chamber to produce noise can become water logged or freeze in place due to condensation in the breath. The chamber of a pea-less whistle is often flat so it takes up less space in your pack or on your survival necklace.

Sounds in *groups of three* are universally accepted as a sign of distress. Blow the whistle three times, yet pause a second between each blast. Sound waves distort over distance and rough terrain so three whistle blasts made in rapid succession can give the illusion of sounding like one.

Failure to give kids signal whistles in the backcountry along with strict parental instruction on how and when to use them in an emergency has no doubt contributed to the needless deaths of dozens of youngsters.

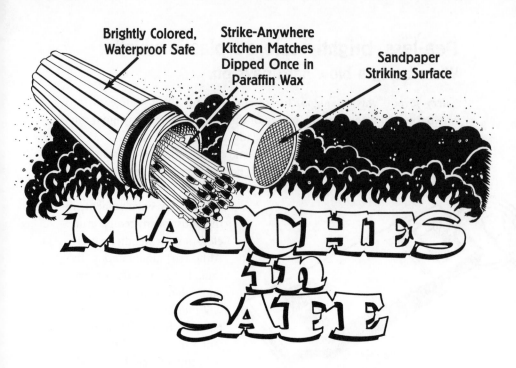

Brightly Colored, Waterproof Safe

Strike-Anywhere Kitchen Matches Dipped Once in Paraffin Wax

Sandpaper Striking Surface

MATCHES in SAFE

Paraffin-coated, strike-anywhere kitchen matches in a brightly colored match safe:
The art of getting hot and bothered without striking out.

The humble match is one of the most awesome inventions ever to grace planet Earth. Nearly every survival kit I've seen or heard about, regardless of the variables imposed on it by its creator, has packed within its depths this simple yet effective tool.

In northern California during the early 1900s, a starving man was caught stealing from a rural slaughterhouse. He appeared to be an American Indian, as he spoke neither English nor Spanish, but none of the local Indians who came to speak with him could understand his language. Big-city anthropologists were summoned to his jail cell and it didn't take them long to realize this was no ordinary guy. A few years earlier, the man had been living in the remote California foothills with members of his tribe, a tribe that had no contact with white people. He called himself "Ishi" and was reportedly the last "wild" American Indian found in the continental United States.

One of the visiting anthropologists ended up taking him to the Bay area to live. Imagine for a moment being jerked from a Stone Age lifestyle to find yourself plopped down in the middle of a city. Even in the early 1900s, the Bay area was a bustling metropolis featuring high-rise buildings and cable cars. Several months into city life, someone asked Ishi what impressed him most about modern civilization. Of all the in-vogue wonders he'd experienced, from central heating to running water to the current transit of the day, he simply replied, "matches." Ishi thought they were truly magical, an amazing invention, and after all these years, he's still right.

In 1680 an Englishman named Robert Boyle, undoubtedly the father of pyromania, discovered that phosphorus and sulfur would burst into flame instantly if rubbed together, uncovering the principle that would ultimately lead to the modern match. A century-and-a half later in 1827, English pharmacist John Walker produced his "sulphuretted peroxide strikables," massive, three-foot-long sticks that would be the predecessors of today's matches. In 1836, the first phosphorous matches were patented in the good old USA and were called, of all things, "locofocos."

Early matches didn't catch on with the general populace because they were incredibly unstable and tended to explode when struck. Improvements were made, yet still the invention didn't catch on. The match finally came into style in America at the end of World War I with the return of our nation's soldiers. It seems they had been using them for months to light cigarettes while fighting from their trenches. I guess an exploding match is nothing in comparison to being shelled and shot at day and night. It's interesting to note that just a few years ago, wooden matches were slightly thicker than they are today, thereby providing more heat for the user. This fact of the incredible shrinking match is yet another testament to the phrase, "They just don't make 'em like they used to."

Strike-anywhere matches are not the same as "safety," or *strike-on-the-box* matches. You can tell the difference by looking at the colors of the match heads. A safety head is only one color, but a strike-anywhere match is two colors: one for the phosphorus and one for the oxidizing agent. This colored tip is highly susceptible to friction and allows you to strike the match on bizarre surfaces such as zippers, fingernails, or rocks in the backcountry. They come in two sizes—one wimpy and pathetic, the other robust and virile. A box of the robust type are individually larger than most any other match on the market and retail for less than two bucks at most grocery stores. They're cheap, widely available (for the time being), may be struck on a thousand surfaces, and can be souped up with candle wax for field use.

Safety matches are such that you actually need the striker on the box to get them to light. When the manufacturer says, "strike on the

box," they mean it. Not even various grits of sandpaper will work. These are unacceptable in survival situations, as they limit you as to where you can strike your match to create fire.

The head of a safety match, invented in Sweden in 1855, contains sulfur and oxidizing agents such as potassium chlorate along with powdered glass, fillers, coloring, and a glue/starch binder. Oxidizing agents are chemicals that take electrons from other chemicals and are necessary to keep a flame lit. The striking surface on a box of safety matches contains red phosphorus (formed by exposing explosive white phosphorus to sunlight or heating it under pressure to above 527°F [275°C]) powdered glass, filler, and binder.

Striking a match initiates a chemical reaction. When a safety match is struck, the friction caused by glass powder rubbing together produces enough heat to cause a small amount of red phosphorus on the box striker to transform into white phosphorus vapor, which catches fire in the air. This tiny amount of heat generates a reaction that uses the potassium chlorate to produce oxygen gas. The heat and oxygen gas then cause the sulfur to burst into flame, catching the wood of the match on fire. In other words, the *oxidizing agent* on the match head is ignited *only* when struck on the *specially prepared combustible striker* on the side of the box.

The heads of strike-anywhere matches contain phosphorus sulfide P4S3, oxidizing agents, powdered glass for friction, and a glue binder. Since the oxidizing agent and red phosphorus are in the same package, these matches can be struck on damn near anything and are not dependent on the box striker. Because of their potential fire hazard, strike-anywhere matches are prohibited on commercial flights and illegal in many countries.

One strike-anywhere match, burned clear through, is the equivalent of a BTU, which is the amount of heat required to bring one pint of water up 1°F (0.56°C). The average human body generates 300 BTUs per hour in metabolic heat. This means that your body gives off more warmth every hour than the equivalent of an entire box of matches. In cold weather, trapping this heat with insulative clothing helps ward off hypothermia.

The chemical components in match heads are highly volatile and degrade over time. Even when stored within airtight containers, the heads still deteriorate. Therefore, you must rotate the matches in your survival kit, ideally every year, two years at the most. If you live in an unusually humid or moist climate, you may need to rotate them more frequently.

The age of a match is also important. If you compare old matches to new ones, which is about as thrilling as watching worms mate, you'll see that the white or blue tips have noticeably degraded. New tips will be bright white or blue; old ones will be pockmarked and faded. Old matches are much harder to light, if they light at all. They typically sputter, smoke, and put themselves out after a few striking attempts. Rotate your matches and this won't happen.

After buying matches, paw through the box, picking the ones with the biggest, fattest heads and most muscular bodies. (Sounds like some folks I know at the gym.) This is anal-retentive but worth it. Matches are not lovingly created by hand by dozens of Old World craftsmen. They're churned out by the millions with little regard as to how they look when they come out. Open a box and see for yourself. Some are a sorry excuse for a match, and look more like a punk-rock toothpick.

After you pick the winners, and there are more winners than you're

How to Coat Your Matches with Paraffin Wax

⬆ Choosing the best matches.

⬆ Removing matches from liquid paraffin wax.

⬆ Drying coated matches "head-up."

⬆ Placing finished matches in match safe.

going to carry in your match safe, put them by the stove and break out the old candles. Melting down candles and coating your matches with paraffin creates a match with a longer burn time and a larger flame. The more heat you have when lighting a fire, the more you can get away with using inferior or damp fuels. Coat the entire match, a few at a time, using something other than grandma's prized cookware. While this doesn't truly make the match waterproof, it does help it repel moisture. Melted paraffin is combustible, so be careful and use a double boiler if necessary. After a few seconds, remove the little guys with tweezers and dry them head up, their bases stuck in a piece of Styrofoam or other suitable substance to keep their heads free from drips. Big, gnarly globs of wax on a match tip may put it out when being struck, or worse, prevent the match from striking at all. I've coated matches once, twice, three times a lady. Anything more than once in the wax seems to be overkill (no pun intended.)

A plain, strike-anywhere kitchen match in a windless environment has a burn time of approximately 30 seconds. Coat it with wax and the burn time increases to nearly 60 seconds. Wax-coated matches carried in a hot environment have the drawback of melting to each other. Regardless of this, I feel the pros far outweigh the cons.

After you've waxed your matches, put them into a match safe. Pack in as many as you can, but not to the point where they can't be removed smoothly when needed. It's easy to get greedy, cramming so many matches into your safe that you'll need a pair of pliers to get them out. This turns the task of obtaining a match into a fine-motor skill, which we know should be avoided. To remove a match, sharply strike the top of the match safe (cover off) into the palm of your hand. This avoids littering the ground with precious fire starters. If you've packed the right amount, this action will usually dislodge one or two from the bunch. If matches are packed too loosely and rattle around as you hike, over time their heads will start to wear down. This is especially true of unwaxed matches. Carrying loose matches while spacing out the need to rotate your stock is a great way to create toothpicks.

Match safes consolidate matches for greater visibility. They also keep matches waterproof, prevent breakage, allow them to float, and protect them from abrasion, wear, and oxygen degradation. Match safes also prevent against a lesser-known occurrence. Every year, seven Canadians die of strike-anywhere matches striking anywhere. Some dude with loose matches in his pocket busts a few moves to impress a babe and before he knows it, his clothing is on fire. Burn enough of the body's largest organ—the skin—and you're vapor. This is a Canadian statistic, so the incident rate is probably higher in the United States. Your match safe should be obnoxiously visible. For God's sake, don't buy one that's camouflaged. They look hip on the bar next to the cheap can of beer but have no place in the field.

How can you tell if your match safe is waterproof? Unfortunately, you have to buy the safe, throw in a match, and submerge it in a glass of water for 30 minutes or so. If your match is dry, it works. Use rubber cement to glue a piece of 400- or 600-grit sandpaper to the bottom of the safe, creating a striking surface. Some people think it's cool to put the striking surface on the inside of the match safe's cap in order to keep it dry. Unless you point the match heads south of the cap, friction could cause one of them to ignite in a closed container with limited oxygen. In other words, you've made your own pipe bomb, minus the pipe. Choose a match safe that's easy to open with cold hands or when wearing heavy gloves or mittens.

There are several specialty matches on the market, including varieties of wind and waterproof, waterproof and paper. Most cost $1.50 or more per box for 20 matches. All of the ones I've checked out must be struck on the box. In other words, if you follow my recommendation of putting your matches in a match safe, you'll need to remove the striker from the box and cart it along with the matches. If you choose to put the striker in the match safe itself, *make sure no match heads come into contact with it* and consider the fact that you've limited your striking options to that particular striking insert. Imagine having dozens of matches and not being able to light any of them because you forgot to bring along a tiny piece of striker material.

While impressive at first, after a few seconds most windproof and waterproof matches become as hot as the sex drive of a 90-year-old man. Most specialty matches are flat-out anemic looking, causing one to wonder when the manufacturers are going to get a clue and beef up the size of their product. One specialty match that's worth checking out is the REI (Recreational Equipment Incorporated) Storm Match. The Storm Match is oversized, even larger than my beloved strike-anywhere kitchen match, and burns like a blowtorch. The box says for outside use only, and they aren't kidding. I struck several indoors and felt similar to what one might feel sniffing lacquer thinner. Once lit, this little beauty can be quickly plunged in and out of water, and more times than not will relight itself and continue burning. Impressive. They are marginally waterproof and can easily handle a few minutes in the drink and still light. Longer soakings require the match to be carefully dried out, as the match head itself starts to become mushy, although this is true of most matches under such conditions. Drawbacks to the Storm

Match include the fact it must be struck on the box or on one of the striking inserts included. The match is longer than conventional matches, requiring it be cut down to fit into a traditional match safe. The Storm Match does have its virtues, but the choice is yours. You might consider carrying a few of them along with your strike-anywhere matches.

Disposable butane lighter (brightly colored, nonopaque, adjustable flame, non-childproof):
Super-fast flame from the field to the heavy-metal concert tribute.

Although most folks consider lighters as trappings of a modern society, the concepts by which they operate—flint, steel, and fuel—have been around cross-culturally for thousands of years.

Lighters, like anything mechanical, are prone to breaking or in some way screwing up. The more moving parts, the greater the chance for error. Yet when they work, they produce our much sought-after flame in one easy-to-do movement. In essence, lighters are fairly simple. One of their inherent beauties is their ability to produce flame with one hand, a gross-motor skill requiring a minimum amount of coordination and physical dexterity. Even when the butane supply is spent or lost, in the hands of a knowledgeable person sparks produced from the striker wheel can be used to create fire, although this is not an option with a piezoelectric type. While lighters are not exactly waterproof, quickly running the striker wheel several times across a flat, nonslick surface should produce enough heat to dry out the element, thereby putting you back in business. Butane lighters will not work if they become cold. Try it yourself. Take your lighter, throw it in the freezer for a couple of hours and you tell me. It doesn't take much to warm the little guy up, but it would suck to find this quirk out in the middle of a snowstorm.

All lighters are not created equal, as there are several on the market, each possessing its own unique attributes. What every good survivor wants is radiant flame—good old-fashioned flames in the campfire. It is an art to take a small amount of heat, a spark or an ember, and baby it into the flame most of us are so familiar with. I love tools that provide radiant flame right off the bat. Matches and lighters tend to do this. For this reason I shy away from fancier windproof lighters that produce heat but no flame. I also shy away from paying 40 bucks for

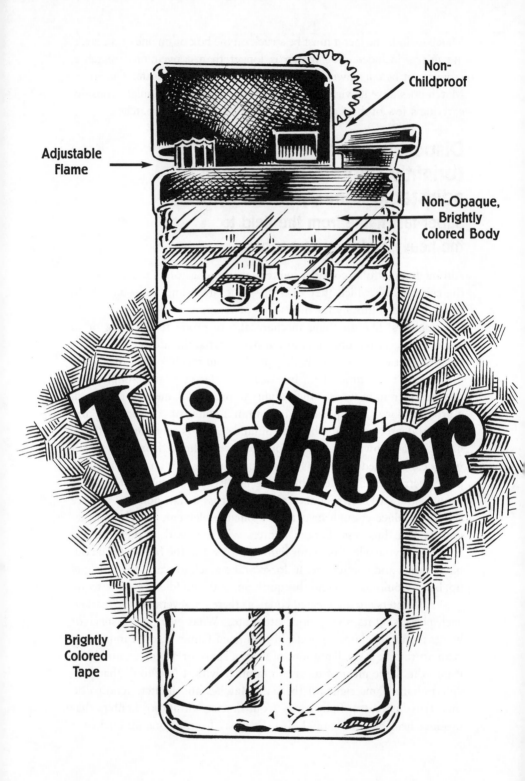

Non-Childproof

Adjustable Flame

Non-Opaque, Brightly Colored Body

Lighter

Brightly Colored Tape

a lighter.

Zippo-brand lighters are quaint, but I don't like them for emergency field applications. Their main advantage is hands-free operation. Once you spin the striker wheel and ignite the fuel, you can set the lighter down and it will continue to burn. On the flip side, they are heavy, they smell, and they require too much fiddling. Zippos remind me of an old car. You have to kick the tires a few times to see if they'll go down the road. While I deeply respect a piece of gear that can be reused, thus saving our landfills from more junk, the biggest reason I dislike Zippos for emergency use is the fact that you have to keep refilling them with lighter fluid. In Arizona, for example, a full Zippo can completely lose its fluid to evaporation in a few days. To make matters worse, the lighter has no visible fuel supply. There are two ways to check if a Zippo has lighter fluid. The first involves trying it out. It should light up by the third try or better. The second method is unique to the Zippo. If it smells like a gasoline-soaked rag behind the seat of a seldom-used 1953 farm truck, it has fluid. How much fluid, God only knows. (I'm not a Zippo hater. The Harley-Davidson collector series is too cool.) However, unless you're willing to babysit and frequently check its fuel level, in my opinion, this lighter has no place in your survival kit.

The average Bic lighter contains 61 minutes of flame with another 90 seconds of residual popping, small blue flame. Don't operate butane lighters for longer than 30 seconds. If you do, the continuous heat will fry out the element. My lighter experiment took several hours to perform, and involved timing the flame, letting the lighter cool down, then timing the flame again. (It was a long night and gives you some insight into my social life.) While the Bic brand is a quality lighter as far as disposables go, I don't carry them. The main reason I don't is that they lack the option for creating an adjustable flame. In other words, you can't make the flame any bigger.

I carry the flatter profile, no-brand lighters for the following reasons. The slimmer profile fits more easily into my kit, especially my mini-kit, which is illustrated later. These lighters typically have the adjustable-flame option and come in a variety of bright colors with non-opaque bodies, so you can see the butane supply within. Many outdoor stores sell this type of lighter right next to the cash register. Try out every brightly colored one they have, looking for the flame that looks like a blowtorch while on the "high" setting. When the chips are down, it's nice to have the option of creating a lot of heat in order to light fire with inferior or damp tinder and kindling. If you can't high grade the best of the bunch from the store, try the following. First, temporarily remove the metal shield from around the mouth of the lighter to expose a small wheel. (Buy the lighter first!) This wheel has many little cogs on its perimeter, and looks much like the tiny gear it is. By turning it gently one way, you can influence how much butane is released, thereby affecting the flame's height. If you're greedy and turn the wheel too much, it won't light, so go easy on the modification. Using this method, there's no guarantee you'll be able to replace the metal shield, so spend the time looking for the winner that needs no modification.

Add brightly colored tape to the middle of the lighter to increase its visibility while leaving the top and bottom untaped to allow for visual inspection of the butane level. Don't count on being able to perform the shake-and-listen routine to see if it still has fluid.

If your lighter is childproof, give it to a child to de-childproof it. Manufacturers have crippled the lighter's simple, gross-motor operation, causing you to have to hop on one foot and sing a song to get flame. I'm aware of three styles of childproofing and all are fairly easy to disable. An 11-year-old kid showed me how.

Aside from visual inspections before each trip to check the fuel level, operate the striker wheel every few months to see if it still lights. Once you've found the lighter of your dreams, put it in your survival kit and don't mess with it. In all the years I've carried lighters, I've had only two that for some reason lost their butane. In both cases, I wouldn't have known had I not left the bottom untaped to allow for visual inspections. Even in arid climates, lighters corrode around their tops. This is typically just surface corrosion, but why take chances since we are dealing with a mechanical object. If you live in the Northwest or other humid places, you might have to rotate lighters more frequently than I do. Regardless, even if your lighter looks like it's in shipshape, retire and replace it with a new one after a few years.

Lighters can act like small bombs when they are exposed to extreme heat sources like sparks. Two deaths I know of regarding rogue lighters involved separate individuals who both happened to be welding at the time. The moral of the story is, for God's sake don't weld with a lighter in your pocket. While the little buggers can be heat sensitive, they've ridden for years in the glove box of my black, non-air-conditioned Jeep with no trouble. Lighters are cheap, multi-use, easy to operate, lightweight, commonly available, and compact. While not a panacea for all problems, they provide a fairly reliable way to instantly create fire, but, like any tool, use them with a healthy amount of respect and common sense.

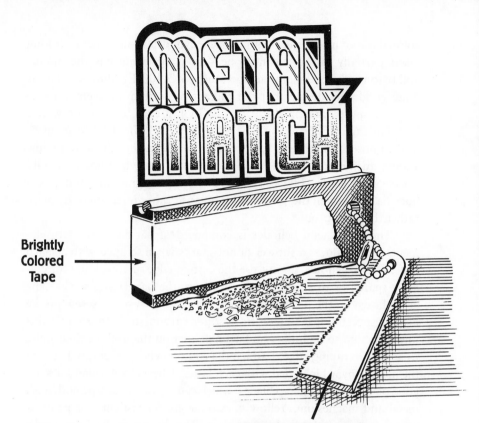

Brightly Colored Tape

Brightly Colored Carbon Steel Hacksaw Blade

Magnesium-block fire starter with hacksaw blade striker:
Getting the most from your 5,400-degree wonder tool.

Fire is one hot commodity and should be studied inside and out, as it creates, sustains, and transmutes, providing incredible power and options for the survivor. There's a reason it's one of the four sacred elements. Of all the multiuse tools available, virtually none eclipse the adaptability and usefulness of fire. That said, it should come as no surprise that I carry several ways to create this awesome element.

I recommend you carry on or around your person three different methods for lighting fire in three different locations. My choices are strike-anywhere kitchen matches in a waterproof safe, a lighter (modified as described earlier), and a magnesium block with striking insert. The magnesium block is a remarkable little tool. It consists of a silver-colored bar of magnesium with a black, cylindrical mish-metal striking insert partially imbedded into one side. Magnesium has the unique ability to reach combustion temperatures of 5,400°F (2,982°C)! This is quite good considering that the radiant heat from an average flame burns at approximately 2,000°F (1,093°C). It even burns underwater! The challenge is figuring out how to light the stuff. In block form, magnesium poses little threat. Reduce it to small shavings, however, while adding an ignition source, and it burns with a white-hot fury. Old Volkswagen engine blocks were made from magnesium, and posed huge hazards when they caught fire because water intensified the blaze rather than put it out.

The mish-metal cylinder is composed of various rare-earth elements and produces a shower of hot sparks when scraped with a sharp edge. Given a choice, do not use the cutting edge of your knife for creating sparks or to shave magnesium from the bar. Doing so, like the goof shown on the package of some brands, will severely screw up the blade, especially if it's made from softer carbon steel. To combat this phenomenon, some folks grind a small area on the back of their knife to act as a scraping edge. I attach the end of a cheap hacksaw blade to the metal lanyard included with each block. Cheesy dollar-day sales are good places to score cheap blades, which can be used to scrape both mish metal and magnesium. Yellow ones offer greater visibility, or paint or tape them to accomplish the same effect. The cheaper the hacksaw blade, the better the carbon steel it's made from, thus the hacksaw itself can be used as the steel in making flint and steel fires, another multiuse gem.

To produce sparks, scrape the mish-metal insert with the *broken edge* of the hacksaw blade. It's fairly sharp and grips more mish metal per scrape, thereby producing greater quantities of heat. Use a long, forceful, quick scraping motion, attacking as much surface area of the mish metal as possible while slightly flexing the blade, like a bow drawn back to hurl an arrow. Flex the blade too much, and your scraper will suddenly become much shorter. Get into the habit of *pulling back on the magnesium block* as you scrape, not pushing forward with the hacksaw blade, thereby keeping the hacksaw static. Doing so will prevent your hacksaw blade hand from rushing forward at the tail end of a scrape and hitting the tinder, causing the finer particles and magnesium shavings, if used, to filter down into the larger tinder. The truly hard core might wish to grind off the hacksaw blade's teeth. The metal just under the teeth is tempered differently from the rest of the blade and will produce even more sparks than the end method described. Directed into adequate tinder, the sparks alone will often achieve combustible temperatures. If not, there's always magnesium, so read on.

Using a Magnesium Block to Start a Fire

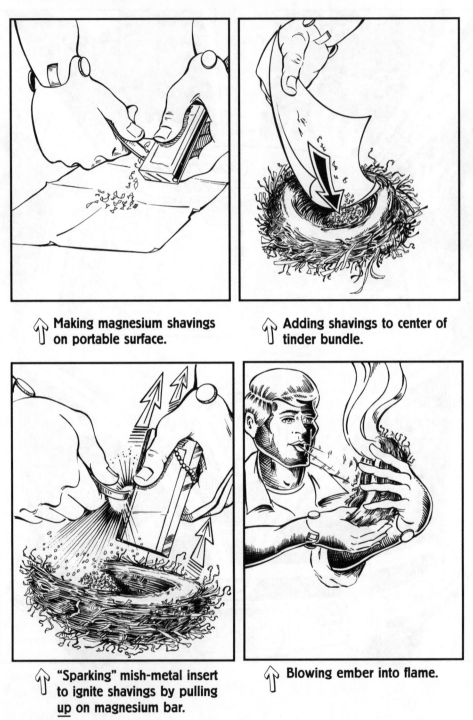

⇧ Making magnesium shavings on portable surface.

⇧ Adding shavings to center of tinder bundle.

⇧ "Sparking" mish-metal insert to ignite shavings by pulling up on magnesium bar.

⇧ Blowing ember into flame.

98.6 Degrees: The Art of Keeping Your Ass Alive!

Magnesium shavings can be added to natural or human-made tinder, producing combustion temperatures very rapidly. To use the magnesium, scrape from the bar as much shavings as needed. One manufacturer recommends creating a pile the size of a quarter. Better overkill than being killed, but accomplishing such a feat will take you the better part of your life. The quality and dryness of your tinder will dictate the size of the pile needed. Wind is a drag, as it blows the tiny metallic flakes hither and yon, so if necessary, seek or improvise a windbreak by forming a slight depression in the ground, stacking a few rocks, or hugging a tree. Scraping magnesium shavings onto a bandana or other portable surface allows you to dump them into your tinder all at the same time. This creates a consistent pile of shavings with all the particles in contact with one another, which is critical to igniting the entire mass at once.

Head to your pre-built configuration of kindling and fuel and carefully place the shavings upon the finest particles of your tinder. Firmly scrape the mish-metal insert with the hacksaw blade, remembering to pull back on the magnesium block, directing the shower of sparks onto the metal shavings. Once lit, they combust rapidly and burn in only a few microseconds. Because of this, as in any fire-building situation, it's important to use the best possible tinder available and build your fire first, before adding the heat or ignition source.

Magnesium tools are cheap and compact. They're available at most camping and discount stores except Wal-Mart (you'll never get past the "greeters" with bare feet). Although mish metal eventually deteriorates when exposed to water for long periods of time, the whole apparatus is waterproof. If you drop the bar into water, simply dry it off and it's ready to use. Creating heat by scraping the mish-metal insert is a gross-motor skill, requiring very little coordination and physical dexterity, which is a definite plus if you have cold hands or are in a panic scenario. As a bonus, the striking insert doubles as a windproof, nighttime signaling device for situations where rescuers possess night-vision technology.

For greater visibility, wrap brightly colored tape around the middle of the block so as not to interfere with the scraping surfaces. As with all survival skills, practice makes a huge difference in performance, so buy two, one to train with and the other to pack away in your kit.

Film Vial

Brightly
Colored
Tape

6 to 8 Triple-Sized
Cotton Balls Slathered
with Petroleum Jelly

Six to eight cotton balls saturated with petroleum jelly in a brightly colored film vial:

Fantastic family fun for creating a cheap, compact, effective, and efficient flaming friend.

Fire lighting can be a real challenge, especially when everything's cold and wet, including you. Since fire is so essential to the survivor, carrying something that makes it easier to light makes good sense. An entire manuscript could be written about the physics involved in achieving ignition temperatures. While I won't go into the finer points in this book, here's the scoop in a nutshell. The more heat you have under your kindling and fuel relationship, the greater success you'll have creating fire, even with damp materials. This "more heat" concept is what quality tinder is all about.

Technically, tinder is any substance that will trap and hold a spark, allowing you, along with the proper combustibles, to nurture it into flame. There are dozens of commercial tinder types on the market, but many have more drawbacks than advantages. Quality tinder should possess several virtues. In an ideal world, your fantasy fire starter should be lightweight, portable, multiuse, cheap, easy to light using gross-motor movements, remain fairly waterproof, and have a long burn time. You should also be able to make it yourself and do so simply. Although this might seem like a lot to ask from tinder, it's a very significant piece of your backcountry gear.

One advantage to commercial tinder is you won't have to spend five minutes making them as you do my homemade stuff. For those with extra time, here's the lowdown on learning to burn.

First, buy cotton balls made from 100 percent cotton. Look for the little cotton symbol on the bag before purchasing. You might already have just what the doctor ordered in your medicine cabinet, so check around the house before you buy. The cotton balls purchased should say "triple size" on the package. Single-sized balls are a joke, having hardly enough surface area to powder a bat's butt. Buyer beware, as there are plenty of synthetic "cotton balls" on the market. Attempting to utilize these impostors for fire-making purposes will alienate you from all your loved ones, as they will melt instead of burn.

Once you've rounded up the balls, grab some petroleum jelly. Yeee-ha! Survival's never been so much fun. Petroleum jelly has the nasty habit of burning like crazy. "Vaseline" is simply a trade name so latch onto the generic version and save some dough. Liberally saturate the outside of the cotton ball with the jelly. Add a healthy amount, about the size of a large grape, and massage it in. Don't rip the cotton ball to shreds attempting to saturate every fiber. Lathering them up to the gills makes the whole contraption harder to light while adding very little burn time.

The finished product should feel like baby snot on the outside but once broken open it will have a central core of dry fiber. These fibers act like the wick of a candle, and the petroleum, the wax. Leaving the central fibers dry allows you to light the ball using gross-motor movement fire-starting tools such as metal matches, magnesium bars, and other spark-producing doodads. As an added bonus, sparks are not blown out by the wind, unlike radiant flames. Dry fibers allow for more efficient lights with matches, too, thus conserving the precious little guys.

To light, simply tear open the ball, expose the dry center, and add an ample amount of heat. Whenever possible, place the ball under whatever configuration of fuel you're trying to burn before lighting. A plain cotton ball will burn for around 30 seconds. Add petroleum jelly and the burn time jumps to five or six minutes! Amazing! During some courses, I have students light fires using half of a paper match, which on an average contains less than six seconds worth of heat. With this homemade tin-der, you now have more than five minutes of heat at your disposal! Remember, the more heat you have, the poorer the fuel and the fewer techniques you can get away with and still start your fire.

I've carried treated cotton balls for years. Old ones light just as well as those freshly made. Another advantage of this multiuse wonder, especially in my arid state, is its use as a topical lubricant, soothing chapped lips, feet, or other body parts. Petroleum jelly also performs well as a marginal grease, reducing friction between surfaces, thereby pro-longing gear life while eliminating obnoxious squeaks.

Store your finished product in a film vial, as these containers are free, easy to find, waterproof, and tough. Cram in as many as you can, usually six to eight. While petroleum jelly does waterproof the cotton (you can drop treated cotton balls into water, pick them up, shake off the excess liquid, tear them open, and light them), it makes sense to put this valuable fire-starting aid into a waterproof case. In addition, the film vial floats if you drop it into the lake or other wet stuff. Cover the vial with obnoxiously colored tape available at your local hardware store, making it easier to spot if misplaced.

Having a tinder source that's ready to light at a moment's notice can make the difference between life and death. Preparedness is a good thing, so stack the deck in your favor whenever possible.

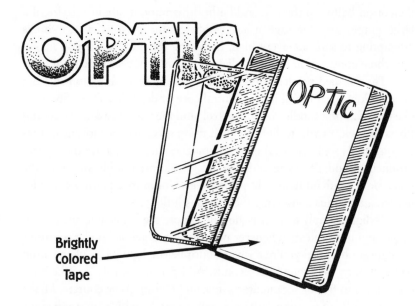

Brightly Colored Tape

Credit-card-sized magnifying lens in brightly colored sheath:
A sound alternative to torturing ants.

Because fire is sacred, carry several means to light it, including the simple magnifying glass or Fresnel lens. Fresnel lenses come in a variety of shapes, sizes, and materials. I recommend you pack the plastic one that's the size of a credit card. Available from many office-supply stores, swap meets, or book retailers, this amazing piece of plastic takes up no space, adds virtually no weight to your kit, and costs less than two bucks. And, of course, it's a multiple-use item. Outside of condensing short-wave radiation from the sun, thereby producing heat to create fire, Fresnel lenses can discern details on topographical maps, unearth hundreds of glochids and cactus spines permeating your epidermis from a desert adventure, or assist in locating foreign matter in the eye.

Using a Fresnel lens to create fire is a bit more complex than torturing ants. Suffice it to say, the more direct and stronger the sunlight, the better results you'll have. In North America in the wintertime, the earth receives less *insolation,* or incoming solar radiation. Thus, in the winter, it's a bit tougher for this device to create enough heat to reach combustion temperatures.

Start by holding the lens at a slight angle in direct sunlight several inches from whatever you're trying to burn. The angling will cause the pattern of magnified light to appear as a half-circle upon your tinder. Slightly rotate the lens until the pattern becomes a full circle. Now, carefully move the lens up and down in relation to your tinder target area until the circle is as small as possible. If done correctly, this pinpoint of intensified sunshine should produce smoke within two or three seconds. Fresnel lenses magnify the sun's rays at only one point in space so it's important to continually micro-move the lens itself, trying to keep the circle of light as small as possible for maximal heat. You're trying to produce enough temperature within a small area of tinder to form an orange "cherry," an ember that sustains itself. Every once in awhile, shade the tinder (it makes it easier to see if there's an ember) and gently blow to see if a cherry has formed. If it has, continue to blow and nurture the small ember into a flame.

I've carried credit-card lenses for years, usually in some compromising place in my fanny pack. Over time, (many years) the edges of the lens start to crack, eventually causing it to break in half. Even so, as long as you have 50 percent or more of the lens intact, it will still focus enough sunlight to create fire in the hands of a knowledgeable person. Most credit-card lenses come with a protective sheath. Unless it's blaze-orange or yellow, cover it with colored tape to increase visibility. *Do not* leave your Fresnel lens lying around outside of its sheath in direct sunlight. I know folks who have stored large glass containers of drinking water in their car on sunny days and have the circular burn marks on their carpet to prove it. Don't underestimate the power of condensed sunlight!

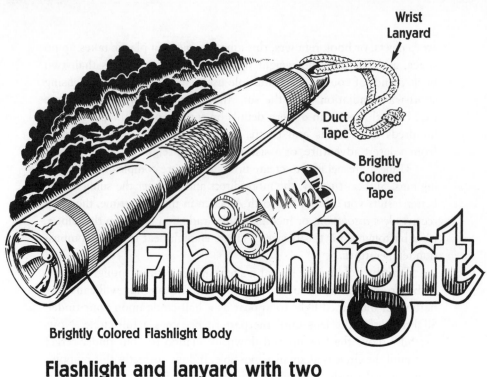

Wrist Lanyard

Duct Tape

Brightly Colored Tape

Brightly Colored Flashlight Body

Flashlight and lanyard with two AA batteries (brightly colored):
Improvised light for the night for minimal fright.

Being able to see in the dark is a gift. Flashlights have saved me more than once from having to spend an unplanned night out in the bush. Once I was snow-tracking a mule deer high in the Arizona mountains. The buck I was following knew it was being tailed and led me on a one-way journey only deer know about. It became dark, I was lost, and a light snow began to fall—not a good situation. I had survival-kit items with me but preferred not to have to spend the night. Using my flashlight, I backtracked and managed to find my way out. A few years ago, I lived in the woods and much of the time I didn't use a flashlight. I became accustomed to the pitch black and familiar enough with my surroundings that I could navigate by starlight, with a hand or cap brim always in front of my eyes, guarding against the stray, cornea-gouging twig. Walking through the woods off-trail in pitch-black darkness is a rush. It forces you to pay attention to what's happening around you as your senses are attuned to the slightest activity. Grooviness aside, if you decide to try it, have a flashlight with you.

There is little substitute for a high-quality flashlight when the going gets rough. Flashlights pave the way for options that may not be possible otherwise. Checking out that "bump" in the darkness, navigating at night to escape oppressive desert heat, locating misplaced items, gathering fuel wood, and a zillion other uses exist with the simple flashlight. Many Search and Rescue teams employ night-vision devices on their searches. Through the magical eyes of night vision, a simple headlamp in the woods looks like a truck with its high beams on. By sweeping your AA light back and forth upon the ground, that search helicopter hovering a quarter mile away might have you sleeping in your bed that night. AA-battery flashlights are typically cheap and compact, most having enough candlepower to get the job done for the average wilderness traveler.

Choose the most dependable, brightly colored flashlight possible or make it that way. In addition, mine sports multiuse military, 100-mph duct tape wrapped around the end as a bite piece. I often hold my flashlight in my mouth, thereby freeing my hands for various tasks. (Teeth and aluminum don't mix, especially when it's 5 A.M. and you're riding a mountain bike down a rocky dirt road.) Retailers sell an array of gadgets meant to anchor small flashlights, including a plastic thingamabob that goes in your mouth, a headband, and a cute little object that looks much like a 1970s Cootie toy. They all serve only one function, and thereby break the cardinal rule of multiuse gear. Over the olive-drab military tape, I've applied the same bright yellow tape I spread on everything else. We are a visually oriented culture, so making your gear strikingly obnoxious is a bonus. At the end of my light is a lanyard that allows me to secure it to my wrist. The lanyard comes in handy in deep snow, heavy brush, and thickets of catclaw, a southwestern shrub renowned for tearing small chunks of flesh from people's bodies. The flashlight I carry is widely available, cheap, has easy-to-obtain spare bulbs, stores a spare bulb in its end cap, and has an adjustable beam. There are some very cool LED lights on the market that spit out a surprising amount of light for their size and have a tremendous battery life. Some are poorly designed for rigorous outdoor use, so use caution and explore what works for you.

Two spare AA batteries with date of purchase:
Extra juice means a lot more use.

Brightly Colored Tape with Date

Spare batteries carried in my survival kit for one year give approximately four hours of light, with the first three being the brightest. The last hour is marginal—it's the kind of light you'd use to read a bad romance novel in your tent on a moonlit night. When replacing the batteries, which is something you should do every year, bind them together using—you guessed it—brightly colored tape. Use permanent marker on the tape to write the month and year they were purchased, as this takes the guesswork out of when you should rotate them. Make sure to change the batteries in your flashlight as well, not just the spares.

It's amazing how quickly the ends of batteries corrode, even in the arid Southwest, so get in the habit of inspecting your spares before heading into the backcountry. If you live in a wet climate, plan on rotating them more frequently. Although the corrosion can be scraped off the ends in a pinch, it's a safer bet to replace them entirely. As a bonus, AA batteries can be placed end-to-end and used in conjunction with super-fine steel wool to quickly achieve ignition temperatures. For whatever reason, Duracell-brand batteries seem to last longer in cold weather than the Energizer brand. Sorry, bunny.

Extra carbon-steel knife with sheath:
Cutting-edge technology from the Stone Age to the space age.

It's interesting to note that in current American culture cutting edges and fire have become synonymous with criminal activity. Both tools are deemed troublesome, and are used simply to help unsavory characters destroy, rob, pillage, and rape. Today, knives are largely misunderstood, thanks to a combination of Hollywood, tool modernization, and irresponsible, blade-wielding thugs. Decades ago, they were an accepted part of our society, even in elementary schools. Every so often, an old-timer attending one of my lectures pipes in with the fact that when he was young, he was supposed to have a knife at school. Years back, young boys were expected to have a blade in order to whittle during recess. My, how things have changed! A knife at school now will earn your expulsion for harboring a dangerous weapon. While I'm not advocating kids at school have knives, I am bringing to light how recently our nation's mindset has changed regarding one of the greatest tools of all time.

Paleoanthropologists have proven that early hominids have been diddling around with rocks to create cutting edges for more than 2.6 million years. These edges, whether primitive or modern, have built every civilization on Earth, including the very structure you live in. Face it, a tool that's been around this long deserves your full attention. Cutting edges can be improvised or found in a multitude of forms. Broken glass, sharpened bone or antler, can lids, and a plethora of stones used by ancient peoples around the globe are just a few examples waiting to be exploited by the attentive survivor. If you're prepared and have a survival kit, your cutting tool of choice, at least for most of North America, will be the metal knife.

Perhaps no other piece of survival gear is as hotly debated as the knife. I can already smell the testosterone wafting off the pages. Not unlike matches, it shows up on every survival kit list. However, most survival books rarely get into detail about the knife itself, offering little information other than to carry a "good pocketknife." On the other hand, some instructors have a vested interest as they sell or endorse blades for a particular knife maker.

It's no secret that knives are phallic symbols. Some guys think the bigger the better . . . whatever works. The *Rambo* movies pretty much sum it up. In each sequel (unfortunately there were two), Stallone's knife gets bigger, harder, and more ridiculous looking, the final blade resembling a futuristic sword more than a knife. Maybe bigger is better for some, but no matter how big your tool, it means little if you don't know how to use it. (She doesn't have the heart to tell you, so I will.) On my field courses, I've seen everything from butter knives to full-blown, John Holmes–sized survival knives. It would seem that picking a winning style of knife has as many variables as there are maggots in a road kill.

So what is the best knife to carry in the bush? My answer is whatever you're most proficient in using that accomplishes the greatest number of tasks for your bioregion. As with the survival kit, there is no one knife suitable for every situation. There are, however, certain guidelines you can follow that will minimize the amount of fecal matter you'll have to wade through. As I've said over and over again, simplicity is the key. The more bells and whistles you have protruding from your knife, the more specialized (or useless) it becomes. A simple design is the easiest to use, allowing you to complete the most basic and diverse of tasks while adapting to the greatest number of terrain features. In short, it gives you the most bang for your buck. Survival situations demand you are the jack-of-all-trades; there's no room for specialization. Pack a knife you feel comfortable carrying and using that allows you to accomplish the most. Don't succumb to your or anyone else's inflated ego. There is a time and a place for machetes, but in most of North America, there's not the time nor the place to use them.

My knife choice looks rather boring: no saw back, blood grooves, serrated edges, chrome, or other attachments. The qualities I look for in a general-purpose bush knife that's great for the majority of the planet are as follows:

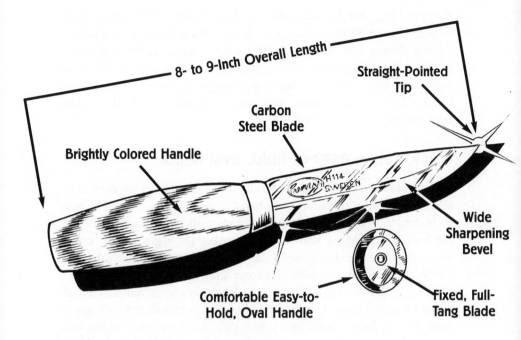

8- to 9-Inch Overall Length

Straight-Pointed Tip

Carbon Steel Blade

Brightly Colored Handle

Wide Sharpening Bevel

Comfortable Easy-to-Hold, Oval Handle

Fixed, Full-Tang Blade

8- to 9-inch overall length

This means the blade itself is about 4 inches long, or the width of your palm. The same is true for the handle. A knife blade of this size lets me skin everything from an elk to a pack rat while performing the majority of backcountry chores. It's comfortable to hold and isn't a drag to carry because it's small and lightweight.

Fixed, full-tang blade

This eliminates folding knives, which are held together by the mercy of a small metal pin that anchors the blade to the handle. This pin is the Achilles heel of all folders, and I've watched more than one blow up in the field when subjected to heavy use. Fixed-blade knives allow you to achieve the power of a small hatchet through the skill of batoning. Although a 4-inch blade has nowhere near the chopping mass of a hatchet, batoning allows you to limb small trees or split wood several inches in diameter by hitting the back of the knife blade itself with a heavy wooden mallet or baton. Simply place your knife upon the appropriately sized material and strike the back of the blade with the baton. This improvised wooden mallet adds the mass missing from a smaller knife and propels the blade through amazingly large chunks of material. Refrain from making the mistake of tackling a piece of wood that's too big, thereby losing the tip of the blade in the material itself as you'll have nothing to hit upon. Attempting to baton with a folding knife is flirting with disaster, as it's simply a matter of time before the pin shears and leaves you SOL. Full tang means the metal of the blade runs clear up into the handle, imparting great strength and control. Hold a knife of this design, and you're actually holding the cutting edge within the handle itself.

Comfortable, easy-to-hold, oval handle

Avoid knife handles with squarish sides or weird protrusions. Even casual knife use with an unforgiving handle can manifest serious blisters. Although, truth be told, prolonged use can create hot spots, regardless of the handle type. Many knives on the market are bogus in this respect alone, sporting hopelessly sharp edges. The phenomenon is extremely common, causing one to wonder if some knife makers bother using their product for more than five minutes. A person's knife handle can tell you a lot about them. If it features sharp edges and their hands are as smooth as a baby's butt, you know they don't use their blade very often, nor could they if they wanted to. A comfortable handle design plays an important role in your ability to safely grip and control your tool, so keep it simple.

Wide sharpening bevel

The bevel of a knife blade is where the rubber meets the road, so to speak, or, in this case, where the metal comes in contact with the sharpening surface. Many knives have pathetic bevels of only a few millimeters in width, making it that much harder to sharpen. Puny bevels force you to gamble with the "one dime, two dime" theory for maintaining the correct blade angle or become a slave to modern sharpening crutches that litter the market. Bowie-knife replicas have huge bevels but feature a tiny functional bevel underneath and are case in point to the fact that we've lost the meaning behind a large bevel.

A friend of mine eats, sleeps, and drinks knives. He can tell you an astronomical quantum about all sharp things and their history—so much so that one beckons the question "Why?" He sharpened a wide-beveled knife I gave to another friend of mine years ago. The end result spoke for itself. While it could shave the hair off a gnat's ass, he totally ignored the true bevel, instead creating his own millimeter-wide one on top of the former. A knife with a wide bevel is a joy to sharpen as you can actually *feel* the bevel "lock in" to the proper angle on the sharpening surface. Even Stevie Wonder could sharpen this knife with confidence.

Straight-pointed tip

Some knife tips turn up, some down. I prefer a tip that's in alignment with the handle, allowing me to effortlessly drive the point into a piece of wood. With the knife firmly anchored, my hands are free to use the blade to cut buckskin lace or whatever. The aligned tip allows the user to pound the knife blade most of the way into a small green tree or shrub. He or she then hits the handle with a wooden baton, going with the cutting edge around the tree, repeating the process as necessary, thereby cutting it down in can-opener fashion if needed.

Carbon-steel blade

Carbon steel is much softer than stainless-steel alloys, making knife sharpening almost pleasant, especially on homemade sharpening boards constructed of wet and dry sandpaper. Because the metal is softer, you'll have to sharpen it more frequently, but at least you'll be able to do so. Treat your knife blade like the scalpel it is! Don't dig with it or, for God's sake, lash it to a pole and try to spear fish as suggested in some survival literature. Instead, use the knife to create a digging stick or sharpen a fish spear.

Carbon steel has another extremely important virtue. As the back of my knife blade has no saw teeth or other protrusions, I can use it to light fire by the flint-and-steel method by quickly striking it along the sharp edge of a hard stone. I'm blessed with the opportunity to make fire from my cutting edge—two tools with which civilizations were built combined into one! Carbon steel discolors with age or when in contact with acids, such as cutting an orange, although I know one instructor who feels this actually improves blade strength. Don't fall into the trap of wanting a shiny toy instead of a tried-and-true, field workhorse. Having a gleaming, stainless-steel blade with metal so hard it must be taken to a shop to sharpen is totally unacceptable. Carbon steel stored wet will seem to rust overnight. While light surface rust is no big deal, as it will be removed with the next sharpening, get into the habit of drying your blade before storing it in its sheath.

Practice, practice, practice

The cutting edge is truly a master creation and will repay you handsomely over and over again, provided you know how to use it. Any tool possessing such power can be a lifesaver in the hands of a knowledgeable person, or a life taker in the hands of the inexperienced. Becoming proficient at using your knife, along with the ability to create fire, are two of the most important skills you'll need. Failure to do so might cause injuries that plunge you into a compromising dilemma in the first place. Take what you want from my opinions and trash the rest. What's important is that you have a knife you like, you know how to use and sharpen it, it gets the job done for your particular geography, and you have it with you in your time of need. As with the other components, make your knife handle and sheath brightly colored by whatever means are convenient.

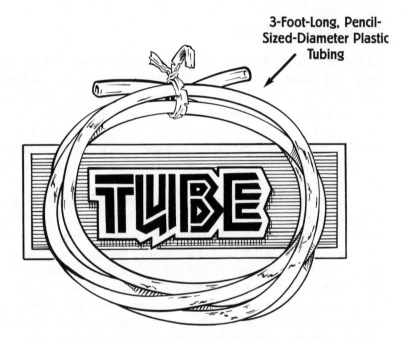

3-Foot-Long, Pencil-Sized-Diameter Plastic Tubing

Clear plastic drinking tube (3 feet long):
The more you suck, the better things seem.

The drinking tube is mandatory desert survival gear, as it's basically a super-long straw, allowing you to harvest water in places where the baggie method won't work. It's common after desert rains to find water trapped deep within the cracks and crevices of rock formations and other hard-to-extract environments. Natural north-facing holding pockets or those shaded by vegetation can contain water for long periods of time, even in blazing temperatures. The drinking tube makes harvesting these natural water caches a breeze. The hardware store has several types and sizes of plastic tubing. Don't purchase a diameter that's too big around or you'll pass out trying to get enough "suck power" to draw liquid up its length. The ones I buy are usually no bigger around than the diameter of a pencil. Three feet seems to be an adequate length for most purposes, and keep in mind that the longer the tubing, the more sucking power is required. Clear tubing allows you to see the action coming up its length, eliminating potential surprises in your mouth, but at this point, who gives a damn. If you have interest, investing in a piece of stretchy, surgical tubing could give you the option of making slingshots and other gizmos.

1- to 2-Gallon Capacity

Collapsible, 1- to 2-Gallon water container:
Properly picking premium plastics and other water-worthy wares.

There are many heavy-duty plastic, collapsible water containers available at decent outdoor stores, but not all are created equal. I have taken at least one well-known brand, filled it with liquid, thrown it, and watched it explode as it skipped across the ground. Obviously, this is not typical behavior in a survival situation. I was simply curious, as the literature the manufacturer provided kept bragging about how tough its product was. It behooves you to purchase a container that's as rugged as possible. Freezer bags are great but don't hold a candle to a well-made, factory-collapsible model. Scout for one that can hold at least a gallon. If you are using halogens for water disinfection, clear containers allow you to see the action and spy unusual substances bobbing about, which can compromise a halogen's ability to kill pathogens. Plastics age with time and become brittle; keep a watch on yours so you can buy a new one when necessary.

In wetter parts of the country, collapsible water containers can be considered optional gear. However, don't forget how sacred water is to regulating body temperature and how handy an extra container can become.

Many possibilities exist for emergency water containers, including oven-cooking bags, balloons, animal parts, gourds, tarps, garbage bags, rain flies, and a host of other nonpermeable barriers. Collapsible containers have the obvious advantage of collapsing, thereby becoming a minimal nuisance in regard to space and weight considerations when not in use. Don't take unnecessary chances locating water in the backcountry. Know water sources in advance, be able to disinfect the goods, stay hydrated, and Party On!

Two 55-gallon barrel liners or three large-capacity leaf bags (store rolled up in a 1-gallon freezer bag):
Having a bash while you crash in your shelter made for trash.

As I said before, the biggest cause of dying in the outdoors is failure to regulate body temperature. In hot, cold, or wet climates, shelter is of prime importance. Barrel liners are truly amazing. Cutting the seam at the bottom of at least one and duct-taping it together makes an extremely roomy tube tent that reaches several feet in length. Barrel liners are typically constructed from a heavier plastic (up to 2.2 millimeters) and are a good choice for your kit. Try the discount and hardware stores for availability. Three large-capacity leaf bags (39-gallon size) will suffice if you can't find barrel liners. You may even prefer carrying leaf bags. I carried them for years. They're not quite as strong but still provide good protection.

Plastic was created on the eighth day. Many, many creations can be made with plastic, a cutting edge, duct tape, and ingenuity.

55 gallon Barrel liners

Gallon-Sized Freezer Bag Container

Potential candidates include, but are in no way limited to, rain suits, water collectors, moisture-proof ground tarps, shade and rain shelters, cordage, signal panels (if brightly colored), containers, glue, pack straps, belts, and a countless variety of other goods. Any material that is wafer-thin, cheap, lightweight, portable, durable, simple to obtain, holds water, and easily sheds rain, snow, and wind at whatever pitch you desire is truly an amazing substance. Wow, talk about a multiuse product! Making a shelter using natural materials in North America requires a lot of work for it to shed rain. I lived in a pine forest for two years in a brush shelter. Due to the poor thatching materials available, I had to be very careful about the pitch of my shelter so it would shed precipitation. This is not a factor with plastic. Building with plastic saves a ton of time, calories, and body water; it's a smart choice for the survivor.

All plastics are vapor barriers, meaning they will not let water vapor escape. Instead, water molecules become trapped and collect on the surface, looking much like dew. This fact could be compromising in certain outdoor situations, as it may cause clothing to become wet with perspiration if not properly vented. As cool as the stuff is, plastic has its drawbacks, so experiment in the backyard before the backwoods. As stated above, if you can latch onto those big, brightly colored bags used for highway clean-up programs, your shelter or rain suit will double nicely as a highly visible signal panel. Most all plastics become brittle with age, so remember to rotate your liners every year or so. Storing them rolled up within a gallon-sized freezer bag keeps the liners clean and free from scratches caused by sand, twigs, and other abrasive grit settled at the bottom of your kit.

Brightly Colored Exterior

Heavy-duty space blanket (brightly colored):
More fun with physics through reflected radiation.

While not as reflective as its smaller cousin, the heavy-duty space blanket is much more durable. These blankets are constructed of a tougher woven material and have grommets in the corners. For a few bucks more than the original design, you could proudly own the model with the built-in hood, thereby protecting the all-important head and neck area. The hooded model also features hand pockets sewn into two of the corners, allowing you to easily wrap the blanket around your body. Although smaller than a tarp, they're useful for shelters, ground cloths, windbreaks, or a simple body wrap. On summer desert-survival courses, they're the only shelter I carry; they work great for escaping sudden monsoon thunderstorms, and provide just enough reflected warmth for reasonable comfort despite plummeting nighttime temperatures.

Heavy-duty space blankets possess only one reflective side. The flip side comes in a choice of colors. Purchase the blaze-orange model for dual use as a signal panel. If orange is hard to come by, red makes a good second choice. Heavy-duty space blankets feature many of the same properties as the smaller model, so I won't waste space repeating these virtues.

Wool or synthetic stocking cap (brightly colored):
Functional fashion for the great outdoors.

Of all the body's areas that lose and gain heat, the head and neck are the most critical. Your head is like a smokestack, and continually loses or gains radiation—and if left unprotected can lose up to 70 percent of your body's total heat production. The human brain needs a constant supply of blood sugar or glucose; thus the blood vessels don't "shunt," or constrict, as much in response to cold weather as those within other parts of the body. The vascular structure of the head is exposed and lacks an insulating layer of fat. This is one time when being a fat head would pay off. In addition, unless you're a member of the Hair Club for Men, hair provides little insulation value in weather extremes. In cold-weather conditions, donning a quality hat is the equivalent to putting on a light sweater. In frigid weather, remember that the face is part of the head, too, and the combined heat loss from it and the respiratory tract can lose up to one third of your body's heat production!

Exposing the head to scorching desert temperatures and direct solar radiation can rapidly cause overheating and increase dehydration.

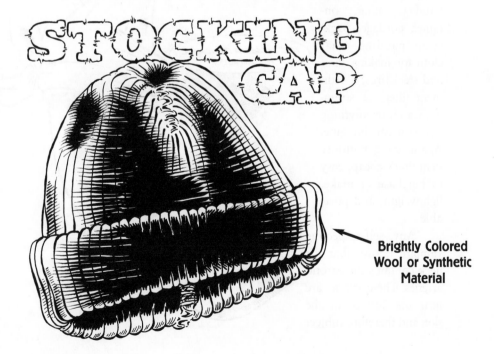

Brightly Colored
Wool or Synthetic
Material

During hot temperatures, a wool or synthetic hat can be dunked in liquid, thereby cooling the user through evaporation. Aside from producing shade for your head, wool is a renowned insulator. Insulation, or dead air space, is an advantage in hot *and* cold weather. Your junior-high lunch box Thermos did the same thing when it kept your soup hot or the lemonade cold.

Remember: you're trying to thermoregulate body temperature. This neat little piece of gear is lightweight, commonly available, cheap, compact, and works in hot and cold climates. It simply covers a part of your anatomy that's crucial to your well-being. Packing a hat that's obnoxiously colored allows it to double as a visible signal to rescuers. It's the perfect excuse to break out that butt-ugly, yellow-and-fluorescent-orange polka-dot hat your aunt gave you for Christmas in '72.

Cotton bandana (brightly colored):
A multiuse joy no gang member should be without.

A bandana is useful for billions of tasks. It's a potholder, head-band, scarf, hat, a filter worn over the mouth against dusty or cold air, washcloth, signal flag, bandage, sling, container, cordage, pack-strap padding, char cloth for making flint-and-steel fires, a sediment filter for straining water, or anything else you can imagine. Again, it's a multiuse item that's cheap, easy to purchase or make, lightweight, and portable.

IT'S CALLED A BANDANA... ... YOU FRUIT!!

Any self-respecting vampire knows that the neck contains the carotid arteries. These arteries are near the surface of the skin and therefore subject

98.6 Degrees: The Art of Keeping Your Ass Alive!

to heat loss or gain through outside temperature extremes. Wrapping a bandana around your neck in cold temperatures helps reduce heat loss, while covering your neck from summer sun reduces heat gain. I carry a cotton bandana year round, although as I've mentioned, it's not the best material for cold, wet environments. If you wish, carry an acrylic, quicker-drying bandana in the winter and a cotton bandana in the summer for its superior cooling effect when wet. If you frequent winter environments, slap a few bucks down for a nice piece of brightly colored wool fabric and make your own.

Cotton material, when properly prepared, has the ability to transform itself into char cloth. True char cloth will catch and hold the tiniest spark. In the hands of an experienced person, this spark can be nurtured into flame using a tinder bundle. Having a brightly colored bandana gives you the option of using it as a flag, panel, or other signaling device, enhancing your attraction value to rescuers.

100 feet of 550-pound-test parachute cord (white color for summer, olive or black for winter): Exploring the sacred virtues of one fiercely fabulous fiber.

Quality cordage (rope, string, etc.) is an incredible asset to the survivor. For thousands of years, indigenous peoples around the globe literally tied their worlds together. Buttons were a drag to make and Velcro and zippers were still things of the future. These people prepared and twisted natural fibers to carry babies, hunt food, transport water, and manufactured clothing and shelter, shoes, weapons, fire, and a limitless array of tools. In our modern society of too much too soon, the ancient art of cordage is still going strong, as it is used in everything from tents and clothing to boot laces and seat covers for your car.

Cordage is a big deal, as it can be used and is useful for many things. While making cordage by hand from plant and animal fibers is doable, it's very tedious. Since you have the opportunity to carry fiber that doesn't require any personal calories or water to make, why wouldn't you? Knowledge is power, yet a survival scenario is no game, so plan ahead by carrying quality modern cord.

In my opinion, nothing says "good morning" for the outdoor traveler quite like military, 550-pound-test parachute cord. It is truly a wondrous piece of backcountry gear. I carry at least 100 feet of the

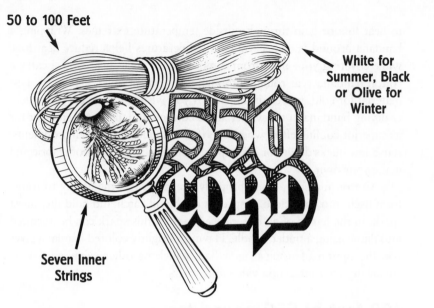

50 to 100 Feet

White for Summer, Black or Olive for Winter

Seven Inner Strings

sacred string but admit that I'm a cordage junkie. I recommend that you carry at least 50 feet. It's rarer than common sense to find, as modern-day parachutists have switched to more efficient flat straps made from Spectra, Dacron, or Vectran. Check your local military surplus store and similar catalogs to locate the fabulous fiber.

The true beauty of 550 cord rests beneath its outer-colored sleeve, which in itself is a great cord. This sleeve houses *seven individual pieces of string*. In other words, if you're carrying 10 feet of 550 cord, you're actually packing 80 feet of viable product for the same amount of space, weight, and cost. Amazing!

Some folks sell 550 cord that isn't. Squish the potentially fraudulent fiber between your fingers. If it feels loose, like it's missing a few internal strings, it probably is. The easiest way to tell fake cord is to simply cut off the end and count the inner strings. Beware of certain brands that use the phrase "para" within the title of their product. They simply use the phrase to confuse hapless buyers into believing it's the real deal. These impostors are manufactured from one piece of braided material. The disadvantage of buying this type of cord is obvious, as when you have 10 feet of the stuff, that's all you have. It can't be broken down into smaller strings without sacrificing length. I've seen 550 cord rip-offs in blaze-orange, purple, and many other colors. Even so, if you can't locate the goods, buy some of the fake stuff as it's still higher quality than the crap being pawned off at the discount stores.

To separate the fibers for individual use, cut off a quarter inch from each end and gently and slowly pull one of the strings free.

Although somewhat messy to accomplish and not recommended for very long pieces, doing so allows you to save string, yet satisfy whatever needs you have, such as binding together a shelter or stitching a hole in your sweater.

Parachute cord is made from nylon. Nylon frays, so melt the ends with a match or lighter before packing. This same meltdown quality allows for emergency patch jobs, using the bubbly goo to mend a variety of tears and punctures on an assortment of surfaces. Genuine U.S. military 550 cord typically comes in three colors: black, white, and olive drab. White is easier to see when dropped on the ground during temperate months, while black and olive show up well on snow.

I once called an East Coast company looking for a deal on the fiber. The folks at the other end of the phone turned out to be a huge industrial complex that custom-made cord for military and private sectors. They coolly asked me how many hundreds of spools I wished to order. I coolly told them I'd get back with them. Click.

Glass, Sightable

Duct-Tape-Reinforced Foam Pouch

Three-by-five-inch glass, sightable signal mirror with brightly colored duct-tape-reinforced pouch:
An excuse to be obnoxious through signaling for rescue.

In a survival scenario, getting rescued is the name of the game. One of the most useful tools for signaling for rescue is the signal mirror. Signal mirrors are routinely visible from 30 to 40 miles away, with some epic accounts of more than 100 miles. Having a tool that can reach out and touch someone at those distances for less than ten bucks is a must-have. In the late 1800s, a mirror in the form of a heliograph helped the U.S. Army catch Geronimo, that hell-raising Apache so dear to my heart. Regardless of one's physical prowess and cunning, it's difficult to outrun light rays.

Using a Sightable Signal Mirror

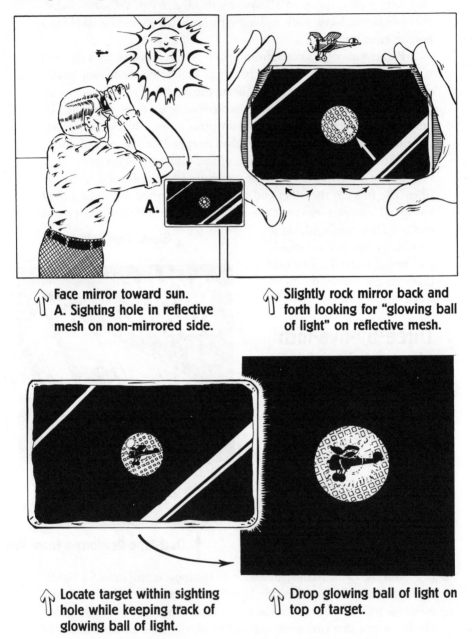

A.

↑ Face mirror toward sun.
A. Sighting hole in reflective mesh on non-mirrored side.

↑ Slightly rock mirror back and forth looking for "glowing ball of light" on reflective mesh.

↑ Locate target within sighting hole while keeping track of glowing ball of light.

↑ Drop glowing ball of light on top of target.

There are several reflective signaling devices on the market, most of which bite the big one. In order to be found, you want as much light as possible reflecting into the eyes and surroundings of your rescuers. Dust and debris in the atmosphere, hazy cloud cover, and a number of other variables rob your reflective device of its shine power, impeding it from reaching its intended destination. Although I've even heard of polished knife blades being used to attract attention, you want to pack the most reflective conventional surface possible, which is silver-coated glass, a.k.a. mirror. Notice that I said glass. There are several synthetic, acrylic impostors available at outdoor shops. Shining the reflection of a glass mirror next to the reflection of an acrylic mirror is all the proof you'll need. The glass one cranks out a crisp, obnoxiously bright reflection. The acrylic imposter is blurred and dull by comparison. Yes, real mirror is heavier to lug around and breakable, but it's your butt that's on the line.

If possible, carry a 3 x 5-inch glass, Air Force–style sightable signal mirror, available at most large outdoor stores. It comes inside a cheesy foam pouch, so beef it up with your friend and mine, professional-grade duct tape. Applying brightly colored tape over the duct tape increases the unit's visibility. Although you can create improvised reflections with your vehicle's rearview mirror—and you should know how to do so—having a "sightable" mirror allows for much greater accuracy in hitting your proposed target.

Students in my courses sometimes wonder what the big deal is as they can flash a tree and see the reflection just fine. That's cool if rescuers are 50 feet away. As soon as the student tips the reflection toward the sky, however, he or she instantly understands the importance of a quality sightable mirror. All of a sudden, that tiny reflection on the tree bark disappears into thin blue sky. You are *not* going to see the reflection off the airplane you flash. Mathematically speaking, the farther you are from the target, the greater your chance is of not hitting the objective. It's similar to orienteering with a map and compass. Screw up even a few degrees with the compass and the farther you travel, the more off you'll be as the mistake grows exponentially.

The style of signal mirror I recommend is mirrored on one side with a circle of reflective mesh in its center. Within this mesh center is a small sighting hole. Oriented properly, the direction in which the mirror is aiming sunlight corresponds directly to a *glowing ball of light* appearing on the reflective mesh. The glowing ball moves whenever you move the mirror. Describing how to use a signal mirror with words is as about as effective as the war on drugs, but here's an attempt.

How to Signal for Rescue

1. Hold the mirror close to your face and orient it toward the sun while looking through the sighting hole in the reflective mesh. (*Don't* look directly into the sun.)

2. Slightly move the mirror in all directions to find the glowing ball of light reflected off the mesh. Notice that the glowing ball moves when-ever you move the mirror.

3. While keeping track of the glowing ball, look at your rescue airplane, Jeep, or people through the sighting hole in the reflective mesh.

4. Move the mirror until the glowing ball of light drops into the sighting hole *on top* of the object you're trying to signal. Remember: the glowing ball *is* where the mirror is aiming reflected sunlight, so dropping this ball on top of your target is the name of the game.

5. Once you've hit your target, slightly rock the mirror back and forth, creating flashes of movement to cover the entire target area. This further eliminates your chance of missing the mark, as a static reflection on the fender of your would-be rescuers' four-wheel-drive vehicle might go unnoticed.

Your ultimate goal is to blast the person in the face, creating enough movement and reflection that you can't help but be noticed. Make sure your rescuers see you, but don't be a jerk about it. A circling airplane rocking its wings knows where you are. Continuing to ricochet a beam of sunlight through the plane's cabin and into the pilot's face is not recommended. The reflection from a mirror can achieve so much distance that it actually wraps around the curvature of the earth, so even if no rescuers are within sight, continue to flash the horizon line. If your situation permits, stay with the vehicle (plane, car, boat, or other), as it provides a much larger target area for searchers to find as well as offers an abundant supply of survival resources.

Signal mirrors make great companions for folks who wear contact lenses and can aid in removing foreign matter in the eye. The mirror also allows for primping and the trimming of unsightly nose hairs, as you never know if one of your rescuers will turn out to be the babe of your dreams.

Contrast and *movement* are hallmarks of effective signaling. Every signaling option you try should possess at least one of the two, ideally both. On an average, you'll have 30 seconds to signal the airplane you see flying overhead, less in canyon country, so like everything else in this book, learn how to use it before you need it. Please don't practice on real airplanes.

Homemade first-aid kit:
Bandaging the boo-boos while soothing the scrapes.

Contrary to popular fantasy and media hype, most backcountry injuries in the United States stem from common events such as hiking, walking, skiing, etc. Exotic injuries such as shark attacks and avalanches account for less than 4 percent of all deaths. Every person venturing into the bush should have at least basic first aid and CPR training. Those spending

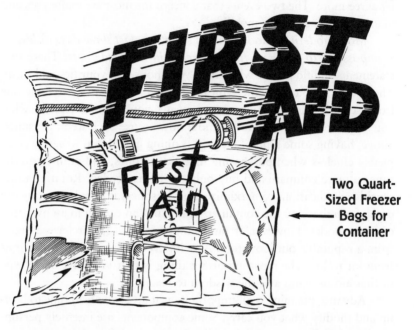

Two Quart-Sized Freezer Bags for Container

more time in the outdoors should invest in Wilderness First Responder (WFR) and/or Emergency Medical Technician (EMT) training. As stated earlier, this book is not meant to be a medical handbook. There's a ton of information on the market regarding wilderness medicine, so I'll touch briefly on the subject.

Seasoned medical personnel, whether urban or wilderness, have a great sense of what's needed and what's not in regard to first-aid supplies. These folks, especially backcountry medics, are tuned into what works for frequently occurring, practical situations. Ask the advice of someone you respect and trust. Many medics in my neck of the woods praise the virtues of Saran Wrap and duct tape and the multiple wonders they achieve. One thing should go without saying: Don't carry supplies you don't know how to use, and treat patients only within the scope of your training. While the "reasonable man" law protects those who are eager to help a victim of circumstance, performing open-heart massage ten miles from the trail head is generally frowned upon.

A recent study suggested that strains, sprains, and soft-tissue trauma accounted for a whopping 80 percent of all outdoor injuries. Viral illnesses or diarrhea caused 60 percent. Not surprisingly, researchers concluded that wilderness first aid should focus upon proper hygiene and the treatment of musculo-skeletal injuries and soft-tissue damage. Having taught hundreds of students in the backcountry for several years, I couldn't agree more. The two events that concern me most are major cuts and injuries that incapacitate mobility.

Most modern outdoor survival situations last three days or less. It is impossible to cover all first-aid needs in the wilderness. These two statements should dictate what items you choose for your first-aid stash. The choice is yours whether you purchase a retail kit or assemble one from scratch. Creating your own means you'll know exactly what you've packed and, hopefully, know how to use each item. As stated above, having some kind of medical training means you won't be completely clueless when purchasing first-aid supplies, and grants you the time to price compare and buy only the items needed. Rotating time-sensitive medications to maximize their freshness is easy by writing the date of purchase on the container. This is not an option in an over-the-counter model. However, if push comes to shove, purchase a setup from a reputable outdoor store. As with everything else, quality varies from kit to kit. The most important thing is that you have some type of first aid on hand and the wisdom to use it.

Advance planning is all-important, as it gives you lead time to beef-up and modify what you carry. Some components are intensely personal and might feature special medications and devices dependent upon the needs of the user. Regardless of limitless variation, three situations wreak havoc with the human body. They are the A, B, Cs, (airway, breathing, and circulation). All three can be extremely hard to deal with in a remote location.

Since I deal with groups of people in the backcountry for a living, my kit contains supplies absent from others. In addition, some items are carried specifically for clients, such as moleskin for blisters and latex gloves for treating open wounds. Generally, I'm concerned about that one big, nasty cut, as I frequently combine knives and heavy chopping tools with folks who have a limited experience with both. Because of this, I pack several dressings, bandages, and first-aid tape. Dressings cover the wound itself while bandages keep the dressing in place. I also carry several different-sized Band-Aids, triple-antibiotic ointment, and medications, including Ibuprofen, Tylenol, aspirin, decongestants, antihistamines, and laxatives. Also squirreled away are some cough drops, electrolyte solutions, tweezers, gauze, and a syringe for irrigating wounds.

Find training that enables you to deal with specific outdoor medical scenarios and stretch the resources you have through the power of improvisation. In essence, your intention behind first-aid supplies should differ little from the concepts we've explored regarding your

survival kit. Pack gear that accomplishes more than one task, such as a large bandana that acts as a compress, a sling, ties for dressings, an eye patch, or a neck warmer. I've created splints from tree branches and duct tape on more than one occasion.

Arizona has the largest variety of venomous creatures in the nation. That said, I pack a "Sawyer Extractor" suction device for nasty bites and stings. I've only had to use it once, but with great success, on a scorpion envenomization. I also carry a couple of specialty items, including a tube of lanolin (a topical lubricant) and Krazy Glue. I use both as first aid for my feet—lanolin on the cracks to promote healing and Krazy Glue if the lanolin fails. Get the Krazy Glue brand, not super glue, as it's a little less caustic on the epidermis. As far as cracks to the epidermal layer, I've also had good results using triple-antibiotic ointment. The petroleum base keeps the tissue supple (and burns like crazy on a cotton ball!) while antibiotics help prevent infection.

I keep the contents of my first-aid kit double-bagged inside two quart-sized freezer bags. The clear plastic allows me to zero in on just the item needed. On the outside of the bag is written "first aid" in permanent marker thereby eliminating confusion if another party were to access the goods. Although, statistically speaking, dying of exposure is your main concern, injuries are very common in a survival situation; 39 percent of them require evacuation.

✱ For new information regarding federal regulations on ephedra use, see page 215

Uncle Peppy's patented power pack stack:
You're weak, weary, and worried but still need to walk.

When you're staring into the face of death, you need every possible advantage to reverse the trend. The following recipe might give you or a loved one the needed energy boost to turn a survival situation into nothing more than a close call. Hundreds of compromising scenarios in the backcountry stem from physical exhaustion and lack of mental alertness. The two states feed off each other like a dysfunctional relationship, causing the affected outdoor recreationist to swirl ever faster down the toilet bowl of apathy. The military has been speeding for decades, and routinely uses otherwise illegal amphetamines, nicknamed "Go-Pills," as "fatigue-management tools." I have my own personal horror stories regarding artificially induced, chemically altered states, and by no means advocate the use of drugs. I don't like ingesting as much as an aspirin but will if there are no other alternatives. The following recipe, like anything else, should be used with a great deal of discretion, common sense, and moderation. All the ingredients at the time of this writing are legal in most states and easy to obtain over the counter without a prescription.

The ingredients in Uncle Peppy's potion are *caffeine* and *ephedrine*. This "thermogenic stack" has been used by body builders for decades to increase the metabolism of body fat. While we as survivors don't give a damn about burning fat (quite the contrary actually), what we're after is the stack's side effect, which is increased physical energy and mental alertness. Whenever two or more drugs are combined, they achieve a completely different result, good or bad. This response is called *synergy*. Combining caffeine with ephedrine results in a completely different stimulant affect than taking one or the other separately.

Nearly 90 percent of Americans consume caffeine in one form or another every day, making it hands down our nation's most popular drug. Caffeine is known medically as *trimethylxanthine,* and when isolated in its pure form is an extremely bitter tasting, white crystalline powder. Mainly, it's used medicinally as a cardiac stimulant and a mild diuretic. The diuretic part is not cool when you're trying to conserve water but caffeine doesn't appear to increase dehydration when taken shortly (about an hour) before exercise, probably because the exercise itself tends to tone down urine production. If you're taking this stack in the first place, it's assumed you're commencing upon the hike of your life, literally. As most every college student studying for finals is aware, caffeine provides an energy boost accompanied by a feeling of heightened alertness. Caffeine pills work better at enhancing performance than coffee because coffee contains chemicals that dull caffeine's physiological effects.

Nearly two decades ago, scientists unearthed the biochemical reason why folks crave a morning cup of java. As the body prepares for sleep, your brain creates and releases a chemical called *adenosine*. Adenosine binds to your adenosine receptors, which cause drowsiness by slowing down nerve cell activity. To a nerve cell, caffeine looks a lot like adenosine, so it binds to the receptor instead. Since caffeine doesn't slow down the cell's activity and hogs all the receptors, the cell speeds up, causing increased neuron firing in the brain. The pituitary gland sees all the commotion and freaks out, releasing hormones that tell the adrenal glands to produce adrenaline. Adrenaline, of course, has a number of effects on your body, including increased heartbeat and the opening of your breathing tubes.

In summary, short-term caffeine use blocks adenosine reception so you feel alert. It injects adrenaline into your system, thereby boosting energy, and manipulates dopamine production to make you feel good. Notice I emphasized *short-term* use. The horrific effects caused by long-term caffeine addiction speak for themselves.

Ephedrine, a close relative of amphetamine, is a naturally occurring stimulant that comes from the Ephedra bush and has been used for centuries. In the 1800s, Mormons used it as a substitute for coffee. In China, ephedrine has been used for more than 4,000 years in the form of Ma Huang. It's sold today as pills, herbal remedies or teas, cold medicines, and inhalers; it's also commonly used as an anti-asthmatic drug, as it stimulates the bronchial passages. Legal in most states, ephedrine can be bought without a prescription in gas stations and drugstores across the country. Many truck drivers working long hauls and students studying late into the night take it to help them stay awake. Ephedrine has recently received bad press because of its abuse in diet and energy products and the over-the-top concentrations used in various concoctions. Several enterprising lawyers even have their own Ephedra Lawsuit Web sites; simply type in how you were heinously wronged, and they'll fight for you. Thanks, guys, for caring, and God Bless America!

Ephedrine is absorbed in the stomach, where it cruises into the bloodstream and reaches the brain. It achieves its peak effect in an hour and may last from three to six hours. Short-term effects are similar to other drugs in the stimulant class, but milder. Users may feel a sense of alertness, energy, excitation, increased heart rate and blood pressure, and the jitters. Abuse the stuff by taking too much and you could enjoy tremors, headaches, insomnia, nausea, vomiting, fatigue, dizziness, chest pain, palpitations, seizures, stroke, heart attack, and death. If any of the following apply to you—high blood pressure, liver, thyroid, or psychiatric disease, pernicious anemia, nervousness, anxiety, depression, seizure disorders, cardiac arrhythmia, prostate enlargement, or you're taking any MAO inhibitor or any prescription drug—don't even think about taking an ephedrine-based product without seeing your doctor first. Beware that ephedrine overdose is sometimes reached by ingesting only two or three times the recommended dose, especially when mixed with caffeine! With this product, more is *not* better. Obviously, ephedrine should be treated with the same respect you'd give any prescription drug.

Beware of using ephedrine if you're taking other medications, as it's impossible to know for sure what effect the interaction will have. Like anything dealing with biology, variation is king so experiment with this combination *beforehand* to see how it affects your personal body chemistry. *Initially, assess your tolerance for the stuff by not taking the full recommended dosage.* Many factors affect the action of drugs, including, but not limited to, mood, body chemistry, other medications or illnesses, and your psychological history. Even a medical professional wouldn't be able to say for sure what effect an interaction would have, so play it cautious. Dosages will vary according to body weight, muscle mass, and how you personally react to the drugs in general. Some people are more sensitive than others. Remember, don't carry anything in your survival kit that you're not intimately acquainted with and prepared to use.

There are many caffeine/ephedrine stack brands on the market. Like anything else, knowing what to look for ahead of time will prevent you from getting ripped off. Check out the label for the amount of caffeine and ephedrine in the product. If it's not listed, you can't be sure you're getting the real deal. Caffeine is found in the kola nut and gurana, among other things, so the label might read "gurana, 180 mg." The amount of caffeine in milligrams (usually 55 mg) should be listed after the product it was obtained from and is the most important piece of information. Instead of the word "ephedrine," the label might read Ma Huang. In general, 120 mg of Ma Huang is equivalent to around 12 mg of ephedrine alkaloids. Find a brand that has an eight-to-one ratio of caffeine to ephedrine and you've found the right stuff.

How much?

Individual human physiology and its reaction to any type of drug is a wild card. Even so, obvious variables dictate how much of the stack you should try, including body mass and the purity of your system. In other words, if you weigh 275 pounds of rock-solid muscle, you'll need more for the desired effect than a 112-pound person. If you're a coffee fiend, drinking several cups a day, you'll most likely require more of the mix as well. A typical dose for a large, healthy male is 200 mg of caffeine with 25 mg of ephedrine. A "more is better" philosophy does not apply to the stack so if the above dosage doesn't ring your bell, you're either a very large person or very tolerant of the drugs. For smaller individuals or females, cut the dosage in half, 100 mg of caffeine with 12.5 mg of ephedrine.

Caffeine and ephedrine can be tweaked in their amounts until the cows come home, all with varying effects. Increasing the caffeine component of the stack might be the way to go if you wish to boost the overall dosage, especially if you're a coffee drinker, but do so only in 50 mg increments and don't exceed 400 mg overall. Increasing the ephedrine to 50 mg can get ugly, and can lead to jitters and nausea, at times with no tangible stimulant effect. Going over the 50-mg mark can lead to feeling mentally spaced out and "uncomfortable." In short, increasing the dosage of ephedrine has little if any benefit other than creating an unpleasant experience.

While large doses of the stack don't cut it, regular, multiple doses throughout the day (no more than three to four in a 24-hour period) seem to work well. In addition, if you can manage it, any amount of sleep between doses intensifies the stimulant effect. Long live the all-powerful nap!

Unfortunately, both caffeine and ephedrine are water hogs. The stack should be taken with a half quart to a quart of water if possible. When you feel the effects of the stack diminish, chugging another half quart to a quart seems to revive the stimulation. Believe it or not, taking too much caffeine can calm you down. Overdo it on the stack and you might find yourself feeling lethargic and sleepy. Drinking a quart of water seems to reverse the trend.

I in no way advocate the abuse of any drug. Consider the preceding information, if you choose to use it, as it is intended, as one more tool in your arsenal to keep you and those you care about alive.

7.5-minute
topographical map and compass:
Finding out for certain if you're really up Shit Creek.

If you know how to use them, a decent map and compass can save you a considerable amount of time and trouble in the outdoors. Either one might provide clues that prevent a survival situation from developing in the first place. The advantage of a topographical map, or "topo map," is that it provides a bird's-eye view of several square miles of land, complete with terrain features and other goodies. The term "7.5-minute map" refers to how much land the map represents, and are the same maps typically carried by SAR personnel. Although you can buy topo maps that show a lot more miles, the more land that's displayed on the same size paper, the less detail is rendered. Once you understand how to read a topo map—again, something you should do before a survival situation—all those little squiggly lines start to form a picture. Mountains and hills seem to spring up from the paper while canyons and arroyos carve deeply into its flatness. After awhile, the map takes on a three-dimensional image of the land you're walking upon, which is precisely the point. A road map is not going to tell you that your pro-

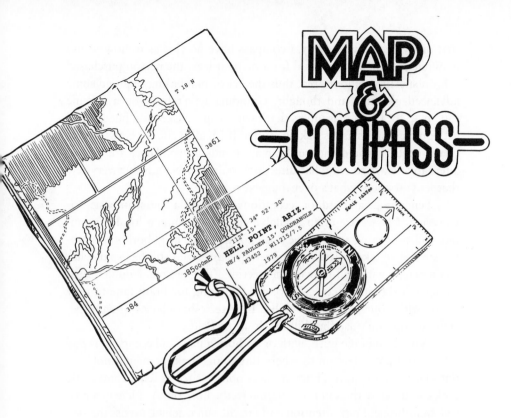

posed route of travel has a 300-foot canyon in the way. Backcountry topographical maps also include many other details, such as waterways, swamps, windmills, cattle tanks, Indian ruins, roads, trails, power lines, mine sites, and ranch houses.

There are dozens of compasses on the market, many with bells and whistles specializing in a certain aspect of orienteering. For most outdoor adventurers, a simple baseplate compass works great in conjunction with a topo map. Many people I know carry a baseplate compass around their neck as part of a wilderness necklace. I also carry a small combination compass and thermometer that hangs from a zipper on my fanny pack. This provides a quick, general-purpose directional bearing without having to unpack the kitchen sink.

Using a map and compass is an art form. Using both effectively will require additional reading and practice from one of the many orienteering books available. It is very easy to get yourself screwed around and end up traveling in exactly the opposite direction you intended to go. For some folks with limited knowledge regarding their use, having a map and compass might provide the false confidence needed to make a bad situation worse. Like cutting edges and fire, both are simply tools and must be used repeatedly in order to gain proficiency. My guess is that many people who carry a compass have no clue as to how to use it. While the same can be said for a map, at least the person purchased it for a specific outdoor area, thus the act of purchasing required some advanced planning and thought. Grandma won't buy you a specific topo map for Christmas unless that's what you've asked for, but she will get you a compass as a stocking stuffer. If I had to choose between one or the other, I would choose the map, hands down. There are several alternative ways to tell what direction you're traveling in but very few that let you know what's over the next ridge.

I encourage all outdoor recreationists to take a course in basic orienteering. Classes are often available cheaply through a local community college, Search and Rescue Posse, or from the neighborhood camping store. I've taken several orienteering classes and still feel somewhat incompetent with full-blown orienteering. The reason: I don't use it enough to stay in practice. It doesn't take long for brain fade to play havoc with your orientation skills. Take refresher classes often, especially if you don't use the skill much in the field.

What I do in the bush, with or without a map and compass, is *pay attention*. I pay attention to where I'm going, making mental notes of unusual terrain features, human-made objects such as fences and cattle tanks, and where the sun is in relation to the horizon. As I live in a passive solar home, I pay attention daily to the sun tracking across the sky. In the wintertime (in North America), the sun hangs low in the southern sky and reaches its lowest point by winter solstice. Over the next several months, the arc of the sun climbs higher and higher until it peaks out during the summer solstice. Watching the sun, paying attention to where it rises, its track path, and where it sets, gives me a sense of direction and provides me with a definite 180-degree flip on my return trip home. In other words, if I start hiking west early in the day with the sun at my back, I know in general that to retrace my steps to the east late in the day, the sun should be at my back again. Tracking the sun also gives an accurate reading of how many hours of daylight remain. Obviously, sun tracking is ineffective in certain parts of the country or on overcast days.

I also pay attention to where I've come from and am frequently looking back over my shoulder as I travel. This acquaints me with how the terrain will look on the way back. If I don't return using the same route, at the very least, it opens my eyes to more turf, allowing me to gain a greater awareness of my environment. When a coyote moves, it doesn't just look straight ahead. Its head and body are in constant motion, taking in and processing as much of its surroundings as possible. It can't afford to pass up life-giving opportunities.

Some people are gifted with a natural sense of direction. Some couldn't find their way out of a paper bag. If you're the latter, pay special attention to your training and the extra steps necessary to stay found in the wilderness. Regardless of your experience, anyone can become lost—or as some like to say, "temporarily disoriented"—in the woods. I consider myself as having an exceptional sense of direction, and I've been lost more than once. The easiest way to not get lost is to stay found every step of the way.

Two candy or nutrition bars:
A little glucose rush for that
final push to save your tush.

Food is not a priority in a modern-day survival situation. Seeing as how the world record for fasting was 72 days, accomplished in a snake-filled, glass coffin no less, skipping a lunch or two seems acceptable. Although hunger is uncomfortable, especially when combined with wilderness stressors such as heat, cold, altitude, bugs, wind, and increased physical activity, food-deprived folks can still function for a long period of time. Most Americans possess extra calories around their middle or elsewhere to go well past the statistical three-day scenario.

In my understanding, the most difficult thing about being hungry is thinking about being hungry. The average person eats one ton of food every year, so for the lion's share of the population, having no food for a few days is not that big of a deal. Granted, day one sucks as well as day two, but by day three the body starts getting the message. Fasting (deliberately not eating) has been around for thousands of years. In some religions it is standard practice. I have fasted several times and if you've never tried it, I highly recommend that you do. Fasts that last longer than 2 or 3 days poop out liver glycogen completely and use up nearly half of the muscles glycogen stores. After this, if the body's still without grub, literally and figuratively, the body synthesizes glucose through our old friend gluconeogenesis. Ketone bodies are then formed by the oxidation of fatty acids that are utilized as energy by the muscles and brain. In a normal-fed individual, ketone oxidation accounts for less than 3 percent of the total energy bill for that person. Longer fasts produce so many ketone bodies that they provide for more than 40 percent of the body's energy requirements and up to 50 percent of the brain's glucose needs. Eventually, the longer the fast, the less glucose the body uses, therefore reducing the amount of cannibalization the body must undergo to support gluconeogenesis. Real-life starvation scenarios, such as the Donner Party in which far more women survived than men, show that women may have a metabolic advantage over the guys. Some factors are apparent, such as a typical lower lean body mass and a higher percentage of body fat, yet other differences are still up for study and speculation.

A relaxing fast where you are sipping a tall glass of lemon water can in no way be compared to a wilderness emergency, but it will give you some answers, at least physiologically and psychologically, about how your body deals with a lack of food. The last thing you need in a survival situation is more unknowns, so anytime you can cut down on the fear factor with simple training and hands-on experience, go for it.

Not unlike the knife argument, food in short-term survival is hotly debated. Some people feel you should fast unless you're capable of harvesting at least your basal metabolic rate in energy or the amount of calories burned doing absolutely nothing. Their argument is that nibbling on little bits of food here and there inhibits the body's response to fully switching over to its reserves. Basal metabolic rate requirements vary widely based on age, sex, muscle and bone weight, and height, so pinning down how many calories you burn sitting on your butt can be a challenge. As an interesting side note, fasts lasting more than 14 days cause the body's BMR to decrease by 21 percent as the body becomes super-efficient with its resources.

Other folks prefer the take-what-you-can-get method, such as a friend of mine who teaches military personnel. After marching around in blazing desert heat for a few days with a Special Forces team, a cottontail rabbit revives the whole crew and they're ready to go. One desert cottontail doesn't go far between eight Navy SEALS but he swears by it nonetheless. Granted, the physical conditioning of this kind of soldier is vastly different from what most people have achieved. Medical research has found that ketone production may come to a screaming halt after eating only 150 grams of carbohydrates per day, so the choice is yours. All in all, there's only one way to know how your body feels under the stress of not having food and that's to try it out for yourself.

That said, consider carrying a couple of high-energy snacks in your survival kit. Most everyone at some point or another has "hit the wall," having burned up their available carbohydrate supply. A little kick of simple sugars and carbohydrates might be all it takes to help drag your tired butt out of a potential deadly scene. More important, working at less than 60 percent of your maximum exertion level uses more fat than carbohydrates, thus helping prevent depletion. If available body carbohydrates are drained, heat production starts to fail and you become hypothermic much faster. To use your remaining fat reserves, carbohydrates *must* be added. Take heed, as these last few sentences have no doubt killed hundreds of people.

Since psychology plays such a paramount role in the world of staying alive, having the psychological comfort of a take-along snack might help calm inner panic, helping the survivor focus on something other than fear. Your food stash might be well spent helping others in your tribe as well. Take note that I'm referring to a snack you happen to have with you. Regardless of psychology, for the vast majority of people, haphazardly grazing on wild edible plants is an entirely different thing. Unless you have the necessary training to positively identify the edible plants in your area, leave the plants alone! As we have discussed in minutia, the stress your body, mind, and emotions will be under are extreme. Expect all fine-and complex-motor skills to go to hell in a hand basket, including your cognitive skills. It is no time to gamble with wild plants and the prolonged preparation that many require for edibility. Furthermore, wild edible plants in general don't taste like pizza, and all foods require water for digestion, especially proteins. If you're short on water, plan on fasting, even if you have access to a case of Ding Dongs. Although some would argue against common sense and statistical proof until the cows come home, if I were to limit you to only one item during your emergency, and you chose food over clothing or water, you will most likely be removed from the gene pool. Remember hypothermia and hyperthermia?

There are more choices of energy bars than fleas on a pack rat, all promising eternal salvation in the land of balanced nutrition. Many taste like dirty socks. Some threaten to loosen teeth if you dare eat them in the cold. Regardless of which energy bar you choose, make sure it takes into account the following.

Foods contain three macronutrients: proteins, carbohydrates, and fats. Each group contains a certain amount of kilocalories (kcal), or units of food energy. Each kilocalorie is equivalent to 1,000 calories and is the quantity of heat required to raise the temperature of 1 kg of pure water 1°C. One pound of body weight equals around 3,500 kcal. At 280 kilocalories a pop, that's nearly 13 Snickers candy bars! The largest energy reserves are found in the largest parts of the body, principally muscle (around 28 kg) and fat (15 kg). On an average, your body contains around 1,200 kcal of carbohydrates, 24,000 kcal of protein, and 135,000 kcal of fat—a veritable bonanza of stored energy!

Survival rations, in their truest sense, should not be considered substitute meals. Their main focus is to provide the survivor with sugar in order to minimize catabolism and dehydration in order to increase survival time. Ideal survival foods possess all three macronutrients—fats, carbohydrates, and proteins—which metabolize at different rates within the body. Fats contain the greatest amount of kilocalories at a whopping 9.3 kcal per gram. Carbohydrates come in second with 3.79 kcal per gram, then proteins with 3.12 kcal per gram. While fats are packed with calories, they take awhile for the body to metabolize into the simple sugars or glucose required for energy. In addition, fats are not well tolerated as an energy source at high altitudes. If your trip involves time spent in thin air, plan on substituting extra carbohydrates for some of the fats and proteins, as carbohydrates are already partially oxidized and require less oxygen from the body to convert into energy—up to 8 to 10 percent less! More than any other nutrient except water, a reduced carbohydrate intake depletes muscle glycogen stores, causing endurance to suffer. **For short-term survival (one to three days), a lack of calories is not nearly as important for performance as a lack of carbohydrates.** Simple sugars and carbohydrates provide fast energy because they metabolize very quickly and are required for the body to be able to access its stored fat deposits. For the long term, however, if not accompanied by certain complex carbohydrates and proteins for stabilization, this quick source of energy leaves your body just as quickly. The result is the infamous sugar crash similar to the one experienced after ingesting a half-gallon of butter pecan ice cream in one sitting.

Proteins are not ideal survival foods, especially in hot climates, for several reasons. If water is scarce, proteins should be avoided, as the metabolism of protein depletes body-water stores. Protein metabolism produces urea, a toxic compound excreted by the kidneys. The more protein you eat, the more water the body devotes to the production of urine in order to rid the body of urea. Eating quantities of protein in a limited water situation hastens death through dehydration long before starvation. However, in a long-term survival scenario where starvation is a possibility, the body consumes protein anyway by catabolizing muscle tissue. Unlike proteins, the metabolism of carbohydrates and fats, to a certain extent, contributes to body-water stores up to 12 to 17 ounces per day depending on the type of diet. Furthermore, the metabolism of protein produces a higher metabolic rate, thus it uses more energy and creates more heat. Regardless of the seeming contraindications, use common sense and adapt to your particular situation. Proteins are a wonderful thing in cold, low-elevation environments that have plenty of drinking water available.

Developed in 1981, the Glycemic Index (GI) is a numerical system for measuring how fast carbohydrates in various foods trigger a rise in blood sugar or glucose. Foods high in fats and proteins don't cause blood-sugar levels to rise nearly as much. The higher the GI number, the greater the blood sugar response. In general, a GI of 70 or more is high, 56 to 69 medium, and 55 or less is low. Until the early '80s, scientists assumed that only digested simple sugars produced rapid increases in blood sugar levels. In truth, many simple sugars don't raise glucose levels any more than some complex carbohydrates, as not all carbohydrates act the same when digested. Foods producing the highest GIs include several of the starchy goodies people commonly devour, including breads, breakfast cereals, and baked potatoes. Even table sugar is low on the GI list in comparison. Low glycemic foods include beans, barley, pasta, oats, various types of rice, and acidic fruits, among others.

Consuming food with a high GI, such as a chocolate-covered powdered donut with glittery purple sprinkles, will cause your blood sugar to go through the roof. In response, your pancreas releases insulin in an attempt to combat rising sugar levels as your body indulges in a sweet-toothed overload on par with the office Christmas party. Proteins contain glucagons. These guys swim around the bloodstream trying to stabilize the blood sugar, helping to prevent the crash your body experiences by consuming simple carbohydrates or sugars alone.

The moral of the story is that the survivor should, if possible, carry a food source containing simple sugars and carbohydrates that jump-start the body immediately. This same food should also possess longer-burning carbohydrates for short-term energy, and fats for sustained long-burning energy. Proteins, with thought given to their disadvantages, should be present as well, thus stabilizing simple sugars and carbohydrates and helping to prevent the crash, as well as providing the body with extra, long-burning fuel.

A perfect example of food combining is "pemmican," an American Indian staple that possessed all three macronutrients: berries for simple sugars and carbohydrates, meat for protein, and fat for fat. All three elements were prepared and mixed together to create the ultimate aboriginal trail food.

Fini

SUMMARY

While proofing the final edits for this book, yet another needless heartbreak story hit the news.

An out-of-state couple drove their rental Jeep down a seldom traveled road in February into one of southern Utah's famous National Monuments—a road that even locals considered barely passable in the best of weather.

As they were simply on a day trip, they brought with them no extra clothing, gear, or food other than a packet of Skittles candy and some sunflower seeds. They told no one where they were going and when they expected to return and drove past the open visitor center to the monument.

Hours later, a snow storm buried their Jeep up to the frame, transforming their day trip into a six-day wilderness survival episode. The 26-year-old male was discovered sunburned, wet, and stumbling down a road by local ranchers. His 27-year-old female companion died of hypothermia. Due to a classic case of lack of preparation, one more family mourns the untimely death of a loved one.

No one *plans* to find him or herself in a survival situation. That's part of what makes survival situations so terrifying. While there are no guarantees in life, let alone in the wild world of survival, advance preparation for any outdoor excursion is priceless.

The verbosity in this book doesn't mean diddly unless you practice what has been preached, although I'm in no way insinuating that you must become a survival psycho in order to make it out alive.

I realize that you might eliminate certain survival-kit components and add others specific to your needs, and I encourage you to do so. Don't carry what you don't believe in!

Although this manuscript is cram-packed with technical detail, always remember the sacred art of simplicity. As with most anything involving nature, regardless of prior training, common sense will carry you far. The wilderness is not for you or against you, she just "is" and it's your job as a survivor to adapt to her. If you find yourself in a life-threatening emergency, calm yourself the best that you can, consider your options, and TRY. Your life is precious. As long as you're warm to the touch and have breath in your lungs, never give up and always remember to "Party On!"

THE AMAZING
"THE DRAWINGS AND PHOTOS ARE REALLY COOL BUT I'M TOO LAZY TO READ THIS BOOK" CLIFF NOTES

1. Statistically speaking, what will kill you first in the outdoors is your core body temperature becoming too cold (hypothermia) or too hot (hyperthermia). Watch the weather before your trip, and be prepared for extremes.
2. The two easiest ways to regulate body temperature in hot and cold weather are adequate clothing and water. Pack extra clothes and stay hydrated!
3. As part of your preparation *before* heading into the outdoors, leave a game plan with two people you trust, which can be forwarded to Search and Rescue personnel if needed. This game plan should clearly state, in as much detail necessary, *where* you are going, *when* you will return, *who* is in your party, *what* you are driving, and *why* you are taking the trip. Stick to the plan you create!
4. Make sure the transportation you use is in good working order and contains emergency gear.
5. Have on your person a quality survival kit relevant to the environment and know how to use it.
6. Know how to signal for rescue quickly and efficiently.
7. Don't take unnecessary chances, rest often, calm down, and maintain a "Party On" attitude!!

If it's COLD outside

- Reduce heat loss: get out of the wind, off the cold ground, and remove wet clothing.
- Put on dry, insulative clothing and seek or make shelter. Pay special attention to protecting your head, neck, and torso.
- Build a fire if necessary. Gather extra wood for the night.
- Drink your water (hot if possible with a few dissolved hard candies or sugar). Clear urine means your body has enough water.
- Eat high-energy foods (carbohydrates) throughout the day.
- Get familiar with your area and "make camp" early before it gets dark.
- Rest and conserve your energy unless you are performing vital tasks or exercising to keep warm.
- Maintain a calm, positive attitude.
- Be prepared to signal rescuers at all times.

If it's HOT outside

- Reduce heat gain: get out of the sun and off the hot ground.
- Protect your body with light-colored, loose-fitting clothing. Pay special attention to the head and neck.
- Wet your clothing if water is abundant.
- Don't move around during the heat of the day.
- Drink your water! If water is plentiful, force yourself to drink until your pee is "clear." Clear urine means your body is fully hydrated.
- Get familiar with your area early and "make camp" before it gets dark, even if you plan on moving during the night when it's cooler.
- Rest and conserve your energy.
- Maintain a calm, positive attitude.
- Be prepared to signal rescuers at all times.

The Gotta-Have-It Stuff

The survival-kit components described in this book are listed on the next page for your convenience. Whether you carry these items or a hybrid of your own creation, a bare-bones kit for dealing with a short-term survival scenario must contain the following ideas. Don't get caught up in the specifics like a certain brand or type of knife. Think instead about the general qualities the cutting-edge (knife) has and make sure it effectively meshes with your overall needs, environment, and skill level. Aside from clothing, water, signaling devices, and a "Party On" attitude, the following ideas are not presented in any set-in-stone order because the order will be dictated by your particular scenario.

Must-Have Concepts for a Short-Term Survival Kit

- Adequate means to regulate body temperature for your environment (clothing).
- Adequate means to create potable water to regulate body temperature for your environment.
- Multiple, effective means for signaling for rescue. (Signal mirrors don't work on cloudy days or at night.)
- A "Party On" attitude.
- A cutting edge.
- Methods to create and sustain fire.
- Cordage (string or rope).
- The determined willingness and know-how to use what you have to its fullest potential.

Survival Kit Components in Cody's Kit

- Two heavy-duty freezer bags.
- Tincture of iodine 2%.
- One condom (non-lubricated).
- Regular space blanket.
- One roll of dental floss.
- Colored surveyor's tape.
- Pea-less, brightly colored plastic whistle.
- Paraffin-coated, strike-anywhere kitchen matches in a brightly colored match safe.
- Disposable butane lighter.
- Magnesium block fire starter with hacksaw-blade striker.
- Six to eight cotton balls saturated with petroleum jelly in brightly colored film vial.
- Credit-card-sized magnifying lens in a brightly colored sheath.
- Flashlight and lanyard with two AA batteries.
- Two spare AA batteries with date of purchase.
- Extra carbon-steel knife with sheath.
- Clear plastic drinking tube.
- Collapsible, 1- to 2-gallon water container.
- Two 55-gallon barrel liners or three large-capacity leaf bags.
- Heavy-duty space blanket.

- Wool or synthetic stocking cap.
- Cotton bandana.
- 100 feet of 550-pound-test parachute cord.
- 3 x 5-inch glass, sightable signal mirror with brightly colored, duct-tape-reinforced pouch.
- Homemade first-aid kit.
- Uncle Peppy's patented power pack stack.
- 7.5-minute topographical map and compass.
- Two candy or nutrition bars.

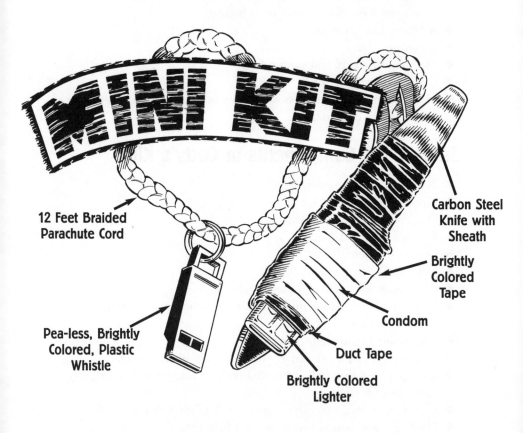

12 Feet Braided Parachute Cord

Carbon Steel Knife with Sheath

Brightly Colored Tape

Condom

Pea-less, Brightly Colored, Plastic Whistle

Duct Tape

Brightly Colored Lighter

NOTE: Other items can be added to customize your survival necklace such as an LED light, small compass, metal match, and so forth.

Choosing the Right Instructor

Many "survival instructors" can be found on the Internet, in print, and elsewhere. Most probably have good intentions, while others see an opportunity for extra income due to the increasing popularity of self-sufficiency training. *It's important that you choose your instructors wisely.* The advice you take dealing with the safety and lives of you and your loved ones should come from a very knowledgeable source. You're learning skills that could save your life—you're not buying a toaster oven. Regardless of an outdoor school's apparent size and media appeal, the number-one variable into the quality of their program is the quality of their instructors.

The following are tips to help you choose a good instructor whether you're looking for skills in outdoor survival, primitive living, or home preparedness. *Remember, any school is only as good as its instructors.*

1. *Ask to see the instructor's resume.* Has your potential instructor been teaching for ten years or ten weeks? In general, self-reliance skills require many years of training and practice before proficiency can be obtained. Ask to see if the instructor has been teaching skills continuously during their self-proclaimed years of operation. It's not uncommon for someone's "30 years of experience" to include the 20 years in the 1970s and '80s when they operated a full-time bug-extermination company.

2. *Train from someone who teaches survival skills full time if possible.* Would you feel comfortable seeing a physician who practiced medicine three months out of the year? Large schools with dozens of instructors have the impossible task of attempting to keep them employed full time. Since finding year-round work in this business can be challenging, locating an instructor that fits this category will tell you something about them—that they are either very good, very lucky, or both.

3. *If your primary interest is primitive-living skills, train from someone who lives in your geographic region.* They will be the most familiar with your local flora and fauna. Learning to harvest cactus fruit from an Eskimo is sketchy at best. If quality concerns you, the longer dedicated instructors have lived within the geographic areas they teach, the greater experience they'll be able to pass on to you.

4. *Ask around about the instructor's background.* Are they known and respected by their peers? Are they in the trenches teaching or just a figurehead for their organization? These days, unfortunately, the school with the best Web-page designer and brochure is thought to be the best wilderness school as well.

5. *Beware the "expert" as nature is too full of variables to support this type of personality.* Large egos and cocky attitudes are all too common in the field of wilderness survival. One of the more unfortunate manifestations of this mindset is the failure to be open to learning new material. Any instructor who tells you there is only one way to do a skill is destined to be upstaged by a humble student who has no preconceived bias as to how that skill is done.

6. *If your interest in learning survival skills runs deeper than experiencing a cool "Eco-vacation," study with someone who knows primitive-living skills **and** modern-survival skills.* Most outdoor schools confuse "modern-survival skills" with "primitive-living skills." Although there is overlap between the two, learning to flint knap a stone knife has limited value for your 59-year-old aunt if she's thrust into a wilderness survival situation. Ultimately, and when taught in the proper order, knowing both sets of skills gives you greater potential for success when dealing with a survival scenario. When the chips are down, a bow drill is no substitute for matches and the know-how to use them.

7. *Before attending a hands-on course, make sure the student-to-qualified-instructor ratio is low.* Unless you're getting a price break, hands-on instruction involving more than ten or twelve students will cause the course quality to suffer because you'll spend more time watching than doing. I specify "qualified" instructors, as large schools often have a heavy instructor turnover rate, and therefore rely on "interns" (future instructors working for free to gain experience). It should go without saying that interns have not yet achieved the field experience and knowledge base of a core, lead instructor.

8. *Is the field course you're thinking about taking really taught in the field or just "outside"?* Training responsibly in a small group allows you to harvest materials directly from the wilderness for maximum learning and enjoyment. A course that supplies all your raw materials could just as easily be taught in a grocery-store parking lot.

9. *You get what you pay for.* If you ever need to use your skills, you'll find them to be priceless.

Happy Training!!

Important Ephedra Update

On December 30, 2003, the U.S. Food and Drug Administration (FDA) banned all dietary supplements containing ephedrine. Initially, in June of 1997, the FDA proposed a statement warning that ephedra should not be used for more than seven days at a time. The new move marked the first time U.S. officials have blocked the sale of an over-the-counter nutritional supplement. The FDA, apparently forgetting about the effects of alcohol and tobacco, stated that " . . . ephedrine alkaloids present an unreasonable risk to the public health and are adulterated and unacceptable under Section 402(f)(1)(A) of the FD & C Act."

According to the Ephedra Education Council, 12 to 17 million Americans use ephedra each year, mostly for weight loss. Over the years, several health professionals have "linked" nearly 100 deaths to the use of ephedra-containing dietary products. Other health professionals have refuted these claims.

Last year, according to the World Health Organization (WHO), more than 430,000 U.S. citizens died out of the more than four million global annual deaths linked to tobacco use. Last year, one in 13 American adults, nearly 14 million people, abused alcohol causing more than 100,000 U.S. deaths. I guess the dietary supplement industry doesn't come close to the congressional lobbying power of big tobacco and alcohol. Even more disturbing is a year 2000 analysis by the FDA linking the drug Viagra to the deaths of more than 500 people seeking the lofty goal of achieving an everlasting erection. Viagra continues to be a bestseller.

Alternative Recipe

The following over-the-counter, alternative recipe should be used with the same rules, respect, and caution as the original Uncle Peppy's formula. A typical dose for a large, healthy male is as follows:

Two Sudafed® nasal decongestant tablets (an FDA-approved over-the-counter decongestant) and one Vivarin® tablet (an FDA-approved over-the-counter caffeine pill).

For smaller individuals and females, cut the dosage in half or take the same amount of Sudafed but use only half of a Vivarin tablet. I realize this contradicts ephedra advice given at the top of page 198. Read the box, do the math, and decide for yourself.

In summary, much like getting out of the bed each morning to participate in life, ephedra use is not without risk. Rather than bowing down in a knee-jerk reaction to media hype and fear, dare to think for yourself. After all, it's one of the first requirements for a healthy, self-reliant mindset.

215

. . . to our web site

for more information about Cody Lundin's
Aboriginal Living Skills School at

www.alssadventures.com

or

Contact us via email: abodude@alssadventures.com

or

Snail mail at: ALSS, LLC
P.O. Box 3064
Prescott, Arizona 86302 U.S.A.

The More You Know,
The Less You Need

Notes
(or tinder)